T0278268

J. I. PACKER

Compiled and Edited by CAROLYN NYSTROM

KNOWING

GOD

THROUGH THE YEAR

A 365-DAY DEVOTIONAL

An imprint of InterVarsity Press
Downers Grove, Illinois

InterVarsity Press
P.O. Box 1400 | Downers Grove, IL 60515-1426
ivpress.com | email@ivpress.com

InterVarsity Press® is the publishing division of InterVarsity Christian Fellowship/USA®. For more information, visit intervarsity.org.

All Scripture quotations, unless otherwise indicated, are taken from the Holy Bible, New International Version®. NIV®. Copyright ©1973, 1978, 1984 by International Bible Society. Used by permission of Zondervan Publishing House. All rights reserved.

While any stories in this book are true, some names and identifying information may have been changed to protect the privacy of individuals.

The publisher cannot verify the accuracy or functionality of website URLs used in this book beyond the date of publication.

Cover design: Anna Poel
Interior design: Beth McGill
Images: Getty Images: © Peter Zelei Images, © Jackyenjoyphotography, © MirageC, © sergio34,
      © YOTUYA, © ulimi

ISBN 978-1-5140-0995-6 (hardcover) | ISBN 978-0-8308-8307-3 (digital) |
ISBN 978-0-8308-4492-0 (paperback)

Printed in the United States of America ∞

Library of Congress Cataloging-in-Publication Data
Library of Congress Control Number: 2015948579

31 30 29 28 27 26 25 24 | 11 10 9 8 7 6 5 4 3 2 1

Introduction

$\mathcal{W}$elcome to the through-the-year devotionals. This small book offers you a wonderful opportunity to reflect each day on the nature of God, drawing near to him in worship, wonder, and praise.

As you begin your journey through the year, talk to God about your motives for reading this book. Thank him that you don't have to earn his approval. Tell him about your desire to grow, and thank him for promising to meet you.

At the bottom of each page, a suggested activity gives you a place to start in responding to the Scripture and accompanying thoughts. That activity may be to reflect, pray, or journal. Because reading without response has little effect, responding to what God has said to you in the daily meditation is important. These suggestions are just a place to start, since meditation and prayer naturally intertwine—one leading to the other.

Beyond that, you may choose to journal. If the reflection raises confusion, you may find it helpful to write your thoughts on paper. Also, some prayers are better written in a journal. A written prayer is just as worshipful as a prayer thought or spoken, and the process of writing gives you a chance to carefully phrase what you say to God—and then come back to it later. Sometimes God will speak to you through reflection and meditation in a way that's so downright stunning that these thoughts should be recorded and read for several days.

These devotions are not dated; you can start anywhere and move around as you please. Most of the reading is condensed and adapted for devotional use from J. I. Packer's *Knowing God*, though not necessarily in the sequence or context of the original book. In addition, several entries dealing with biblical characters come from *Never Beyond Hope* (by J. I. Packer and Carolyn Nystrom). Scattered throughout this devotional guide are quotes from hymns. At the back, you'll find a list of these hymn sources if you want further information on these rich texts of worship and praise.

You'll find a year's worth of devotions here, designed to fill six days a week. We choose to offer six rather than seven, assuming that you will use at least one day a week for worshiping God with his gathered people in your church—and also for a built-in bit of grace as circumstances do sometimes infringe on your devotional time. You can use the seventh day to go back to some of the "pray," "journal," and "reflect" suggestions at the end of each devotional entry.

May you know God more deeply and fully as you focus on his character through this year.

Carolyn Nystrom

WINTER

Monday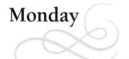

God's Palms

*See, I have engraved you on
the palms of my hands.*

ISAIAH 49:16

What matters supremely is not the fact that I know God but the larger fact that underlies it—the fact that *he knows me.* I am engraved on the palms of his hands. I am never out of his mind. All my knowledge of him depends on his sustained initiative in knowing me. I know him because he first knew me and continues to know me.

He knows me as a friend and is one who loves me. There is no moment when his eye is off me or his attention distracted from me and no moment, therefore, when his care falters. This is momentous knowledge. There is unspeakable comfort—the sort of comfort that energizes, be it said, not enervates—in knowing that God is constantly taking knowledge of me in love and watching over me for my good.

Reflect: *What comfort do you take from knowing that your name is engraved on the hand of God?*

Tuesday

Looking Back—and Up

*Stand at the crossroads and
look; ask for the ancient paths,
ask where the good way is, and walk in it,
and you will find rest for your souls.*

JEREMIAH 6:16

*C*hristian minds have been confused by skepticism. The foundation facts of faith are called into question. Did God meet Israel at Sinai? Was Jesus more than a very spiritual man? Did the Gospel miracles really happen? Is not the Jesus of the Gospels largely an imaginary figure? And so on.

Nor is that all. Skepticism about God has bred a wider skepticism that abandons all idea of unity of truth. Since God is not "out there" in the world but only "down here" in the psyche, uncertainty and confusion about God mark our day.

The prophet Jeremiah voiced the invitation that these devotionals issue. It is not a critique of new paths, except indirectly, but rather a straightforward recall to old ones, on the ground that "the good way" is still what it used to be. Let us join the ancient prophets and the early apostles and walk humbly toward knowing God.

Journal: *How has contemporary skepticism affected your own thinking? What questions do you need answered about God?*

Wednesday

Watchers and Walkers

*Love the Lord your God with
all your heart and with all your
soul and with all your mind.*

MATTHEW 22:37

*I*n *A Preface to Christian Theology,* John Mackay illustrated two kinds of interest in Christian things by picturing people sitting on the high front balcony of a Spanish house and watching travelers go by on the road below. The "balconeers" can overhear the travelers' talk and chat with them, but they are onlookers. The travelers, by contrast, face problems that, though they have their theoretical angle, are essentially practical—problems of the which-way-to-go and how-to-make-it types, problems that call not merely for comprehension but for decision and action.

Take the problem of the Godhead. While the balconeer is asking how one God can conceivably be three, what sort of unity three could have, and how three who make one can be persons, the traveler wants to know how to show proper honor, love, and trust toward the three Persons who are now together at work to bring him out of sin and into glory.

Reflect: *When it comes to knowing God, are you a balconeer or a traveler? Talk to him about it.*

Thursday

Lofty Thoughts

*Such knowledge is too wonderful
for me, too lofty for me to attain.*

PSALM 139:6

At the age of twenty, C. H. Spurgeon proved that he already had his priorities right:

> The highest science, the loftiest speculation, the mightiest philosophy, which can ever engage the attention of a child of God, is the name, the nature, the person, the work, the doings, and the existence of the great God whom he calls his Father. There is something exceedingly improving to the mind in a contemplation of the Divinity. It is a subject so vast, that all our thoughts are lost in its immensity; so deep, that our pride is drowned in its infinity. Other subjects we can compass and grapple with; in them we feel a kind of self-content, and go our way with the thought, "Behold I am wise." But when we come to this master science, finding that our plumb line cannot sound its depth, and that our eagle eye cannot see its height, we turn away with the thought, . . . "I am but of yesterday, and know nothing." No subject of contemplation will tend more to humble the mind, than thoughts of God.

Reflect: *Meditate on God, prayerfully naming his various names found in Scripture. Let yourself feel small in his presence.*

Friday   *Hope for Hurts*

Take my yoke upon you and learn from me,
for I am gentle and humble in heart,
and you will find rest for your souls.

MATTHEW 11:29

C. H. Spurgeon wrote:

> There is, in contemplating Christ, a balm for every wound;
> in musing on the Father, there is a quietus for every grief;
> and in the influence of the Holy Ghost, there is a balm for
> every sore. Would you lose your sorrow? Would you drown
> your cares? Then go, plunge yourself in the Godhead's
> deepest sea; be lost in his immensity; and you shall come
> forth as from a couch of rest, refreshed and invigorated. I
> know nothing can so comfort the soul; so calm the swelling
> billows of sorrow and grief; so speak peace to the winds of
> trial, as a devout musing upon the subject of the Godhead.

We are cruel to ourselves if we try to live in this world without
knowing the God whose world it is and who runs it. Knowing
God is crucially important for the living of our lives.

Reflect: *Picture Christ in any setting recorded in the New Tes-*
tament. Meditate on his work, his character, his teaching. Allow him
to absorb your pain.

Saturday/Sunday   *Shedding Weight*

*Let us throw off everything that hinders
and the sin that so easily entangles,
and let us run with perseverance
the race marked out for us.*

HEBREWS 12:1

You know how Bunyan's pilgrim, when called back by his wife and children from the journey on which he was setting out, "put his fingers in his ears, and ran on crying, Life! life! eternal life!" I ask you for the moment to stop your ears to those who tell you there is no road to knowledge about God, and come a little way with me and see.

Anyone who is actually following a recognized road will not be too worried if he hears nontravelers telling each other that no such road exists. We are in the position of travelers who, after surveying a great mountain from afar, traveling around and observing how it dominates the landscape and determines the features of the surrounding countryside, now approach it directly, with the intention of climbing it.

Journal: *If you were to put your fingers in your ears and run off shouting, "Life, life, eternal life," what would you need to leave behind?*

Monday 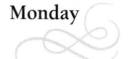 *Motive Check*

*Knowledge puffs up. . . . The man
who thinks he knows something does
not yet know as he ought to know.*

1 CORINTHIANS 8:1-2

$\mathcal{B}$efore we start to ascend our mountain of knowing the things of God, we need to ask ourselves, what is my ultimate aim in occupying my mind with these things? What do I intend to *do* with my knowledge about God once I have it? For the fact that we have to face is this: if we pursue theological knowledge for its own sake, it is bound to go bad on us. It will make us proud and conceited. The very greatness of the subject matter will intoxicate us, and we will come to think of ourselves as a cut above other Christians because of our interest in it and grasp of it. We will look down on those whose theological ideas seem to us crude and inadequate.

To approach Bible study with no higher motive than a desire to know all the answers is the direct route to a state of self-satisfied self-deception. We need to guard our hearts against such an attitude and pray to keep it away.

Journal: *What do you intend to do with your knowledge of God? (Be honest.)*

Tuesday   *Law and Love*

> *Oh, how I love your law! . . .*
> *How sweet are your words to my taste! . . .*
> *Give me discernment that I may*
> *understand your statutes.*

PSALM 119:97, 103, 125

*D*o not all children of God long, with the psalmist, to know just as much about our heavenly Father as we can learn? Is not the fact that we have received a love for this truth one proof that we have been born again? And is it not right that we should seek to satisfy this God-given desire to the full?

Yes, of course it is. But if you look to Psalm 119, you will see that the psalmist's concern to get knowledge about God was not a theoretical but a practical concern. His supreme desire was to know and enjoy God himself, and he valued knowledge about God simply as a means to this end. He wanted to understand God's truth in order that his heart might respond to it and his life be conformed to it.

Reflect: *Reflect on the place of God's law in your life. Do you love it? What do you do with it? How does it reveal God to you? When does it lead you to worship?*

Wednesday

Path Light

*Blessed are they whose ways
are blameless, who walk according
to the law of the Lord.*

PSALM 119:1

$\mathcal{T}$he psalmist was interested in truth and orthodoxy, in biblical teaching and theology, not as ends in themselves but as means to the further ends of life and godliness. His ultimate concern was with the knowledge and service of the great God whose truth he sought to understand. And this must be our attitude too.

Our aim in studying the Godhead must be to know God himself better. Our concern must be to enlarge our acquaintance, not simply with the doctrine of God's attributes, but with the living God whose attributes they are. As he is the subject of our study and our helper in it, so he must himself be the end of it.

We must seek, in studying God, to be led to God. It was for this purpose that revelation was given, and it is to this use that we must put it.

Pray: *How are you a better person because of God's law? Thank God for the times his law has illumined your path.*

Thursday

God Thought

*I meditate on your precepts
and consider your ways.*

Psalm 119:15

*H*ow can we turn our knowledge *about* God into knowledge *of* God? The rule for doing this is simple but demanding. It is that we turn each truth that we learn *about* God into matter for meditation *before* God, leading to prayer and praise *to* God.

What is meditation? Christian meditation is the activity of calling to mind, thinking over, and applying to oneself the various things that one knows about the works and ways and purposes and promises of God. It is an activity of holy thought, consciously performed in the presence of God, under the eye of God, by the help of God, as a means of communion with God. It is a matter of talking to oneself about God and oneself. It is indeed often a matter of arguing with oneself, reasoning oneself out of moods of doubt and unbelief into a clear apprehension of God's power and grace.

Reflect: *Select a topic about God and practice the Christian discipline of meditation as described above.*

Friday

Comfort

Humble yourselves before the Lord,
and he will lift you up.

JAMES 4:10

$\mathcal{T}$he effect of Christian meditation is ever to humble us, as we
contemplate God's greatness and glory and our own littleness
and sinfulness, and to encourage and reassure us. Furthermore,
it serves to "comfort" us—in the old, strong Bible sense of the
word—as we contemplate the unsearchable riches of divine
mercy displayed in the Lord Jesus Christ.

It is as we enter more and more deeply into this experience of
being humbled and exalted that our knowledge of God increases,
and with it our peace, our strength, and our joy. God help us,
then, to put our knowledge about God to this use, that we all
may in truth know the Lord.

Reflect: *Rest in God's presence today. Meditate on his greatness
and his glory, allowing him to place you within his shelter. Receive
his comfort.*

Saturday/Sunday   *Joy*

*Believing, ye rejoice with
joy unspeakable and full of glory.*

1 PETER 1:8 KJV

I walked in the sunshine with a scholar who had effectively forfeited his prospects of academic advancement by clashing with
church dignitaries over the gospel of grace. "But it doesn't matter,"
he said at length, "for I've known God and they haven't."

Not many of us, I think, would ever naturally say that we have
known God. The words imply a definiteness and matter-of-
factness of experience to which most of us, if we are honest, have
to admit that we are still strangers.

Nor, I think, would many of us ever naturally say that, in the
light of the knowledge of God that we have come to enjoy, past
disappointment and present heartbreaks don't matter. Constantly
we find ourselves slipping into bitterness and apathy and gloom
as we reflect on them, which we frequently do. The attitude we
show to the world is a sort of dried-up stoicism, miles removed
from the "joy unspeakable and full of glory" that Peter took for
granted his readers were displaying.

Pray: *Ask God for a joy not connected to events but to himself.*

Monday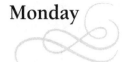

Rejecting Rubbish

> *I consider them rubbish, that I may gain Christ and be found in him. . . . I want to know Christ.*

PHILIPPIANS 3:8-10

*W*hen Paul says he counts the things he lost "rubbish" (or "dung," KJV), he means not merely that he does not think of them as having any value but also that he does not live with them constantly in his mind.

What normal person spends his time nostalgically dreaming of manure? Yet this, in effect, is what many of us do. It shows how little we have in the way of true knowledge of God.

Private mock-heroics have no place at all in the minds of those who really know God. They never brood on might-have-beens. They never think of the things they have missed, only of what they have gained.

"Whatever was to my profit I now consider loss for the sake of Christ," wrote Paul. "What is more, I consider everything a loss compared to the surpassing greatness of knowing Christ Jesus my Lord, for whose sake I have lost all" (Philippians 3:7-8).

Journal: *What prized "possessions" belong on your rubbish heap? Journal a "letting go" prayer. See Philippians 3:4-6 for ideas.*

Tuesday

Incarnation

The Word became flesh and
made his dwelling among us.

JOHN 1:14

*T*he supreme mystery with which the gospel confronts us lies in the Christmas message of incarnation. Here are two mysteries for the price of one: (1) the plurality of persons within the unity of God and (2) the union of Godhead and manhood in the person of Jesus. It is here, in the thing that happened at the first Christmas, that the profoundest and most unfathomable depths of the Christian revelation lie. "The Word became flesh" (John 1:14).

God became man. The divine Son became a Jew. The Almighty appeared on earth as a helpless human baby, unable to do more than lie and stare and wriggle and make noises, needing to be fed and changed and taught to talk like any other child. And there was no illusion or deception in this; the babyhood of the Son of God was a reality.

The more you think about it, the more staggering it gets. Nothing in fiction is so fantastic as this truth of the incarnation.

Journal: *What did Christ give up to come to earth? What did you gain?*

Wednesday

Jesus, Creator God

In these last days [God] has spoken to us by his Son . . . through whom he made the universe.

HEBREWS 1:2

Jesus of Nazareth was as truly and fully divine as he was human. This is the real stumbling block in Christianity. It is here that Jews, Muslims, Unitarians, and Jehovah's Witnesses have come to grief. It is from misbelief, or at least inadequate belief, about the incarnation that difficulties at other points in the gospel story usually spring. But once the incarnation is grasped as reality, these other difficulties dissolve.

If Jesus had been no more than a remarkable, godly man, the difficulties in believing what the New Testament tells us about his life and work would be truly mountainous. But if Jesus was the same person as the eternal Word, the Father's agent in creation, "through whom also he made the worlds" (Hebrews 1:2 RV), it is no wonder if fresh acts of creative power marked his coming into the world, his life in it, and his exit from it. The incarnation is in itself an unfathomable mystery, but it makes sense of everything else that the New Testament contains.

Reflect: *If you were introducing Jesus to a Muslim, what would you say?*

Thursday

Who Is This Child?

> *Out of [Bethlehem] will come a ruler*
> *who will be the shepherd of my people Israel.*

MATTHEW 2:6

*T*he Gospels of Matthew and Luke tell us in some detail how the Son of God came to this world. He was born outside a small hotel in an obscure Jewish village in the great days of the Roman Empire. The story is usually prettied up when we tell it Christmas by Christmas, but it is really rather beastly and cruel. The reason why Jesus was born outside the hotel is that it was full and nobody would offer a bed to a woman in labor, so she had to have her baby in the stables and cradle him in a cattle trough.

The story is told dispassionately and without comment, but no thoughtful reader can help shuddering at the picture of callousness and degradation that it draws. The point of the story, however, lies not in the circumstances of the birth but rather in the identity of the baby. Who is this child?

Journal: *Who is this child? Write your own answer to that question.*

Friday   *John's Purpose*

*These [signs] are written that you
may believe that Jesus is the Christ,
the Son of God, and that by believing
you may have life in his name.*

JOHN 20:31

$\mathcal{J}$ohn knew that the phrase "Son of God" was tainted with misleading associations in the minds of his readers. Jewish theology used it as a title for the expected (human) Messiah. Greek mythology told of many "sons of gods," supermen born of a union between a god and a human woman. In neither of these cases did the phrase convey the thought of personal deity. In both, indeed, it excluded it.

John wanted to make sure that when he wrote of Jesus as the Son of God he would not be understood (that is, misunderstood) in such senses as these. He wanted to make it clear from the outset that the Sonship that Jesus claimed and that Christians ascribe to him was precisely a matter of personal deity and nothing less. Hence his famous prologue of John 1:1-18, which we shall look at in detail in the coming days.

Reflect: *Read John 1:1-18, focusing on various ways that it introduces Jesus as the Son of God.*

Saturday/Sunday

God's Word

God said, "Let there be light,"
and there was light.

GENESIS 1:3

*J*ohn opens his book with the theme that Jesus is the Son of God, but he does so with great care. He does not bring the term *Son* into his opening sentences at all. Instead he speaks first of the Word.

There was no danger of his being misunderstood. Old Testament readers would pick up the reference at once. God's Word in the Old Testament was his creative utterance, his power in action fulfilling his purpose. The Old Testament depicted God's utterance, the actual statement of his purpose, as having power in itself to effect the thing purposed. Genesis 1 tells us how at creation "God said, 'Let there be . . .' and there was . . ." (verse 3). "By the word of the LORD were the heavens made. . . . He spoke, and it came to be" (Psalm 33:6, 9). The Word of God is thus God at work.

Reflect: *"The Word of God is thus God at work." What does this imply?*

Monday

In the Beginning

> *In the beginning was the Word,*
> *and the Word was with God,*
> *and the Word was God. He was*
> *with God in the beginning.*

John 1:1-2

*J*ohn takes up the figure of Jesus as Word and proceeds to tell us seven things about the divine Word. For now, let us consider the first three.

1. "In the beginning was the Word." Here is the Word's *eternity*. He had no beginning of his own. Where other things began, he *was*.

2. "And the Word was with God." Here is the Word's *personality*. The power that fulfills God's purposes is the power of a distinct personal being, one who stands in an eternal relation to God of active fellowship (this is what the phrase means).

3. "And the Word was God." Here is the Word's *deity*. Though personally distinct from the Father, he is not a creature. He is divine in himself, as the Father is. The mystery with which this verse confronts us is thus the mystery of personal distinctions within the unity of the Godhead.

Reflect: *Eternity, personality, deity. A lot is revealed about Jesus in the first sentence of John. Reflect on what it means that this same Jesus is your Savior and your friend.*

Tuesday
In Him Was Life

*Through him [the Word] all things were
made; without him nothing was made
that has been made. In him was life.*

JOHN 1:3-4

*P*icking up on yesterday's devotional, we continue by looking
at two more implications of John's picture of Jesus as Word.

1. "Through him all things were made." Here is the Word *cre-
   ating.* He was the Father's agent in every act of making that
   the Father ever performed. All that was made was made
   through him. (Here, incidentally, is further proof that he, the
   Maker, does not belong to the class of things made, any more
   than the Father does.)

2. "In him was life." Here is the Word *animating.* There is no
   physical life in the realm of created things except in and through
   him. Here is the Bible answer to the problem of the origin and
   continuance of life in all its forms: life is given and maintained
   by the Word. Created things do not have life in themselves, but
   life is in the Word, the second person of the Godhead.

Journal: *Jesus was and is the Creator. Jesus brings and is life.
Throughout this day, look for people, objects, and events that remind
you of this aspect of Christ's being. Make notes of what you find.*

Wednesday

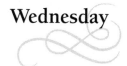

Life and Flesh

In him was life, and that life was the light of men. . . . The Word became flesh and made his dwelling among us.

JOHN 1:4, 14

*J*ohn's description of Jesus as Word has yet more to teach us.

1. "And that life was the light of men." Here is the Word *revealing*. In giving life, he gives light too. That is to say, all people receive intimations of God from the very fact of being alive in God's world, and this, no less than the fact that they are alive, is due to the work of the Word.

2. "The Word became flesh" (John 1:14). Here is the Word *incarnate*. The Word lived among us.

Pray: *Slowly and prayerfully, read verses 4 and 14 of John 1. Meditate on each phrase, then pray your response to God.*

Thursday

Word and Son

*We have seen his glory, the glory
of the One and Only, who came from
the Father, full of grace and truth.*

JOHN 1:14

*F*ourteen and one-half verses into his book, having shown us who and what the Word is—a divine Person, author of all things—John now indicates an identification. The Word, he tells us, was revealed by the incarnation to be God's Son. The identification is confirmed by verse 14, and then in John 1:18 we read, "The only begotten Son, which is in the bosom of the Father" (KJV).

Thus John establishes the point at which he was aiming throughout. He has now made it clear what is meant by calling Jesus the Son of God. The Son of God is the Word of God. We see what the Word is and that is what the Son is. Such is the prologue's message. When, therefore, the Bible proclaims Jesus as the Son of God, the statement is meant as an assertion of his distinct personal deity. The Christmas message rests on the staggering fact that the child in the manger was God.

Journal: *John's prologue is poetic in its revelation of Jesus. Write your own song or poem based on what you see there.*

Friday

Throne of Grace

He had to be made like his brothers in every way. . . . We have one who has been tempted in every way, just as we are—yet was without sin. Let us then approach the throne of grace with confidence, so that we may receive mercy and find grace to help us in our time of need.

HEBREWS 2:17; 4:15-16

$\mathcal{T}$he baby born at Bethlehem was God made man. The Word had become flesh: a real human baby. He had not ceased to be God— he was no less God than before—but he had begun to be man. He was not now God *minus* some elements of his deity but God *plus* all that he had made his own by taking manhood to himself.

He who made man was now learning what it felt like to be man. He who made the angel who became the devil was now in a state in which he could be tempted—could not, indeed, avoid being tempted—by the devil. In fact, the perfection of his human life was achieved only by conflict with the devil. We can draw great comfort from the words of Hebrews quoted above.

Pray: *Meditate on the Hebrews passage above, then allow it to guide your prayer as you approach God's "throne of grace."*

Saturday/Sunday   *Adoration*

> *When Jesus was born in Bethlehem . . . there*
> *came wise men from the east to Jerusalem,*
> *saying . . . we have seen his star in the east,*
> *and are come to worship him.*

> MATTHEW 2:1-2 KJV

The mystery of the incarnation is unfathomable. We cannot explain it; we can only formulate it. Perhaps it has never been formulated better than in the words of the Athanasian Creed. "Our Lord Jesus Christ, the Son of God, is God and man, . . . perfect God and perfect man, . . . who although he be God and man: yet he is not two, but one Christ; one, not by conversion of the Godhead into flesh: but by taking of the manhood into God." Our minds cannot get beyond this.

What we see in the manger is, in Charles Wesley's words,

> Our God contracted to a span;
> Incomprehensible made man.

Incomprehensible. We shall be wise to remember this, to shun speculation and contentedly to adore.

Journal: *Record the words of the Athanasian Creed in your journal, meditate on them phrase by phrase, then write a response of adoration.*

WEEK FIVE

Monday   *Cradle to Calvary*

> *You know the grace of our Lord Jesus Christ,*
> *that though he was rich, yet for your sakes*
> *he became poor, so that you through*
> *his poverty might become rich.*

2 CORINTHIANS 8:9

*H*ow are we to think of the incarnation? The New Testament does not encourage us to puzzle our heads over the physical and psychological problems that it raises but to worship God for the love that was shown in it. The crucial significance of the cradle lies in the sequence of steps that led the Son of God to the cross of Calvary. The key to the New Testament for interpreting the incarnation is not, therefore, the bare statement of John 1:14 but rather the more comprehensive statement of 2 Corinthians 8:9. Here is stated not the fact of the incarnation only but also its meaning. The taking of manhood by the Son is set before us in a way that shows us how we should ever view it—not simply as a marvel of nature but rather as a wonder of grace.

Journal: *Meditate on the notion suggested by 2 Corinthians 8:9, noticing the terms* you *and* your. *Draw a symbol beside each phrase. Pray in response to what this reveals.*

Tuesday

Emptying

[Christ Jesus] made himself nothing,
taking the very nature of a servant,
being made in human likeness.

PHILIPPIANS 2:7

What did Jesus give up when he became human? Does the phrase "made himself nothing," together with the statement of 2 Corinthians 8:9 that Jesus "became poor," throw some light on the nature of the incarnation itself? Does it not imply that a certain reduction of the Son's deity was involved in his becoming man?

This is the so-called kenosis theory, *kenosis* being the Greek word for "emptying." The idea is that in order to be fully human, the Son had to renounce some of his divine qualities; otherwise he could not have shared the experience of being limited in space, time, knowledge, and consciousness that is essential to truly human life.

But the kenosis theory will not stand. When Paul talks of the Son as having emptied himself and becoming poor, what he has in mind (see context) is the laying aside not of divine powers and attributes but of divine glory and dignity, "the glory I had with you before the world began" (John 17:5).

Pray: *Pray to better understand that Jesus "made himself nothing" for you.*

Wednesday

Father and Son

*I have come down from heaven
not to do my will but to do the
will of him who sent me.*

JOHN 6:38

*P*art of the revealed mystery of the Godhead is that the three Persons stand in a fixed relation to each other. The Son appears in the Gospels not as an independent divine person but as a dependent one, who thinks and acts only and wholly as the Father directs. It is the nature of the second person of the Trinity to acknowledge the authority and submit to the good pleasure of the first. That is why he declares himself to be the Son and the first person to be his Father. Though coequal with the Father in eternity, power, and glory, it is natural to him to play the Son's part and to find all his joy in doing his Father's will, just as it is natural to the first person of the Trinity to plan and initiate the works of the Godhead and natural to the third person to proceed from the Father and the Son to do their joint bidding.

Reflect: *Reflect on the mystery of God as Trinity. In prayer, express some of your reflections, bowing in worship.*

Thursday

The Father's Will

*No one knows about that day or hour,
not even the angels in heaven, nor
the Son, but only the Father.*

MARK 13:32

*J*esus did not do all that he could have done, because certain things were not his Father's will for him (see Matthew 26:53-54). Jesus did not consciously know all that he might have known but only what the Father willed him to know. For instance, the reason he did not know the date of his return was not that he had given up the power to know all things at the incarnation. The reason was that the Father had not willed that he should have this particular piece of knowledge while on earth prior to his passion. So Jesus' knowledge was limited by the will of the Father for the Son while on earth. In our moments of frustration over our limited earthly understanding, we can recall that the Son of God was subject to the will of the Father just as we are.

Reflect: *Reflect on what earthly limitations might have meant to Jesus as he followed his Father's will—for you. Give him thanks.*

Friday

The Son's Gift

Do you think I cannot call on my Father, and he will at once put at my disposal more than twelve legions of angels? But how then would the Scriptures be fulfilled?

MATTHEW 26:53-54

We see now what it meant for the Son of God to empty himself and become poor. It meant a laying aside of glory (the real kenosis). It meant a voluntary restraint of power. It meant an acceptance of hardship, isolation, ill treatment, malice, and misunderstanding. It meant a death that involved such agony—spiritual even more than physical—that his mind nearly broke under the prospect of it (see Luke 12:50 and the Gethsemane story). It meant love to the uttermost for unlovely human beings so that they, through his poverty, might become rich.

The Christmas message is that there is hope for a ruined humanity—hope of pardon, hope of peace with God, hope of glory—because at the Father's will Jesus Christ became poor and was born in a stable so that thirty years later he might hang on a cross. It is the most wonderful message that the world has ever heard or will hear.

Reflect: *Reflect on the generosity of God's gifts through Jesus as represented from Advent to Easter. Give thanks.*

Saturday/Sunday

Like Jesus

*Your attitude should be the
same as that of Christ Jesus.*

PHILIPPIANS 2:5

*T*he spirit of Christ is the spirit of those who, like their Master, live their whole lives on the principle of making themselves poor— spending and being spent—to enrich their fellow humans. They give time, trouble, care, and concern to do good to others (and not just their own friends) in whatever way there seems need. There are not as many who show this spirit as there should be.

If God in mercy revives us, one of the things he will do will be to work more of his spirit in our hearts and lives. If we desire spiritual quickening for ourselves individually, one step we should take is to seek to cultivate this spirit. "You know the grace of our Lord Jesus Christ, that though he was rich, yet for your sakes he became poor, so that you through his poverty might become rich" (2 Corinthians 8:9). "Your attitude should be the same as that of Christ Jesus" (Philippians 2:5).

Journal: *What if this picture of imitating Christ were to take place in your life? in the life of your church? What would it look like? If you are willing, pray to that end.*

- 38 -

Monday  *Feeling Free*

You will know the truth, and
the truth will set you free.

JOHN 8:32

*I*f asked how one may know God, we can at once produce the right formula: that we come to know God through Jesus Christ the Lord, in virtue of his cross and mediation, on the basis of his word of promise, by the power of the Holy Spirit, via a personal exercise of faith. Yet the gaiety, goodness, and unfetteredness of spirit that are the marks of those who have known God are rare among us—rarer, perhaps, than they are in some other Christian circles where, by comparison, evangelical truth is less clearly known. Here, too, it would seem that the last may prove to be first and the first, last. A little knowledge *of* God is worth more than a great deal of knowledge *about* him.

Pray: *Pray that you will know God himself, not just about him. Ask God to grant you an unfettered spirit.*

Tuesday

Everything We Need

His divine power has given us
everything we need for life and godliness
through our knowledge of him.

2 PETER 1:3

*O*ne can know a great deal about godliness without having much knowledge of God. There is no shortage of books on church book tables—or sermons from pulpits—on how to pray, how to witness, how to read our Bibles, how to tithe our money, how to be a young Christian, how to be an old Christian, how to be a happy Christian. It is possible to learn a great deal secondhand about the practice of Christianity. Moreover, if one has been given a good bump of common sense, one may frequently be able to use this learning to help floundering Christians of less stable temperament regain their footing and develop a sense of proportion about their troubles, and in this way one may gain for oneself a reputation for being quite a Christian leader. But have we known God? And because we have known God, do we find that the unpleasantness we have had, or the pleasantness we have not had, through being Christians does not matter to us?

Reflect: *Think about the questions raised above, then pray your response to God.*

Wednesday

Energy for God

*The people that do know their God
shall be strong, and do exploits.*

DANIEL 11:32 KJV

*T*hose who know God have great energy for God. Energy for God is exactly what we see happening in the narrative chapter of Daniel, where we are told of the "exploits" of Daniel and his three friends. When King Darius suspended the practice of prayer for a month, on pain of death, Daniel not merely went on praying three times a day but did so in front of an open window so that everyone might see what he was doing (Daniel 6:10).

It is not that Daniel was an awkward, cross-grained fellow who luxuriated in rebellion and could be happy only when he was squarely "agin'" the government. It is simply that those who know their God are sensitive to situations in which God's truth and honor are being directly or tacitly jeopardized. Rather than let the matter go by default, they will force the issue on men's attention and seek thereby to compel a change of heart about it—even at personal risk.

Journal: *What energizes you? Thank God for that capacity. Consider ways you could use your energy for his glory.*

Thursday

Energetic Prayer

> *We do not make requests of you because we are righteous, but because of your great mercy. O Lord, listen! O Lord, forgive! O Lord, hear and act! For your sake, O my God, do not delay, because your city and your people bear your Name.*

DANIEL 9:18-19

*T*he invariable fruit of true knowledge of God is energy to pray for God's cause. This energy, indeed, can find an outlet and a relief of inner tension only when channeled into such prayer. And the more knowledge, the more energy!

Perhaps we are not in a position to make public gestures against ungodliness and apostasy. Perhaps we are old or ill or otherwise limited by our physical situation. But we can all pray about the ungodliness and apostasy we see around us. If, however, there is in us little energy for such prayer and little consequent practice of it, this is a sure sign that as yet we scarcely know God.

Pray: *Pray your way through the news. As you consider how to pray, draw on your knowledge of God, what glorifies him, what his compassions and causes are. Ask that he lead you to pray for people and causes according to his will.*

Friday

Great Thoughts of God

O Lord, the great and awesome God,
who keeps his covenant of love . . .

DANIEL 9:4

*T*hose who know God have great thoughts of God. The central truth that Daniel taught Nebuchadnezzar is the truth that "the Most High is sovereign over the kingdoms of men" (Daniel 4:25). God foreknows all things, and his foreknowledge is foreordination. He, therefore, will have the last word, both in world history and in the destiny of every person. His kingdom and righteousness will triumph in the end, for neither men nor angels shall be able to thwart him. These were the thoughts of God that filled Daniel's mind, as witnessed by his prayers.

Is this how we think of God? Is this the view of God that our own praying expresses? Does this tremendous sense of his holy majesty, his moral perfection, and his gracious faithfulness keep us humble and dependent, awed and obedient, as it did Daniel? By this test we may measure how much or how little we know God.

Journal: *Write your praise to God. Use great thoughts and great words to worship your great God.*

Saturday/Sunday   *Being Bold*

> *Neither count I my life dear unto myself,*
> *so that I might finish my course with joy.*

ACTS 20:24 KJV

*T*hose who know God show great boldness for God. Daniel and his friends were men who stuck their necks out. This was not foolhardiness. They had measured the risk. They were well aware what the outcome of their actions would be unless God miraculously intervened, as in fact he did.

This is precisely the spirit of all who know God. They may find that choosing the course is agonizingly difficult, but once they are clear on it, they embrace it boldly and without hesitation. It does not worry them that others of God's people see the matter differently and do not stand with them. (Were Shadrach, Meshach, and Abednego the only Jews who declined to worship Nebuchadnezzar's image? Nothing in their recorded words suggests that they either knew or, in the final analysis, cared. They were clear as to what they personally had to do, and that was enough for them.) By this test we may measure our own knowledge of God.

Journal: *Who have you admired (past or present) who took great risks for God? Record their names, their deeds, and your thankfulness for them.*

Monday

Courageous Contentment

*Since we have been justified
through faith, we have peace with
God through our Lord Jesus Christ.*

ROMANS 5:1

Those who know God have great contentment in God. There is no peace like the peace of those whose minds are possessed with full assurance that they have known God, and God has known them, and that this relationship guarantees God's favor to them in life, through death, and on forever. This is the peace that Shadrach, Meshach, and Abednego knew—hence the contentment with which they stood their ground in the face of Nebuchadnezzar's ultimatum.

Their reply is classic (Daniel 3:16-18): "O Nebuchadnezzar, we do not need to defend ourselves before you in this matter." (No panic!) "If we are thrown into the blazing furnace, the God we serve is able to save us from it, and he will rescue us from your hand, O king." (Courteous but unanswerable—they knew their God!) "But even if he does not"—if no deliverance comes—"we want you to know, O king, that we will not serve your gods." (It doesn't matter! It makes no difference! Live or die, they are content.)

Reflect: *What is your level of contentment? On what is it based? Pray about your findings.*

Tuesday  *Finding God*

> *"You will seek me and find me when
> you seek me with all your heart."*
>
> JEREMIAH 29:13

*D*o we desire knowledge of God? Then two things must follow.

First, we must recognize how much we lack knowledge of God. We must learn to measure ourselves not by our knowledge about God, not by our gifts and responsibilities in the church, but by how we pray and what goes on in our hearts. Many of us, I suspect, have no idea how impoverished we are at this level. Let's ask the Lord to show us.

Second, we must seek the Savior. The Lord Jesus Christ is now absent from us in body, but spiritually it makes no difference; still we may find and know God through seeking and finding Jesus' company. It is those who have sought the Lord Jesus till they have found him—for the promise is that when we seek him with all our hearts, we shall surely find him—who can stand before the world to testify that they have known God.

Reflect: *Are you a God seeker? Ask God to reveal himself to you as you walk through the ordinary details of your day.*

Wednesday

Perspective

"For I know the plans I have for you,"
declares the LORD, "plans to prosper
you and not to harm you, plans to
give you hope and a future."

JEREMIAH 29:11

*W*hat are we made for? To know God. What aim should we set ourselves in life? To know God. What is the "eternal life" that Jesus gives? Knowledge of God. What is the best thing in life, bringing more joy, delight, and contentment than anything else? Knowledge of God. What, of all the states God ever sees man in, gives God most pleasure? Knowledge of himself.

In these few sentences we have seen a great deal. Our point is one to which every Christian heart will warm, though the person whose religion is merely formal will not be moved by it. What we have said provides at once a foundation, a shape, and a goal for our lives, plus a principle of priorities and a scale of values.

Journal: *Read each of the five questions above and review answers commonly found among your acquaintances. Then write your own honest answers. Pray about the results.*

Thursday

Nothing Tastes?

*This is eternal life: that they may
know you, the only true God,
and Jesus Christ, whom you have sent.*

JOHN 17:3

The world today is full of sufferers from the wasting disease that Albert Camus focused as absurdism ("life is a bad joke") and from the complaint that we may call "Marie Antoinette's fever," since she founded the phrase that describes it ("nothing tastes"). These disorders blight the whole of life: everything becomes at once a problem and a bore, because nothing seems worthwhile. But absurdist tapeworms and Marie Antoinette's fever are ills from which, in the nature of the case, Christians are immune, except for occasional spells of derangement when the power of temptation presses their minds out of shape—and these, by God's mercy, do not last. What makes life worthwhile is having a big enough objective, something that catches our imagination and lays hold of our allegiance, and this the Christian has in a way that no other person has. For what higher, more exalted, and more compelling goal can there be than to know God?

Journal: *Journal some of your own bouts with absurdism and Marie Antoinette's fever. How can (or does) knowing God ease that pain?*

Friday

God's Depths

Oh, the depth of the riches of the
wisdom and knowledge of God!
How unsearchable his judgments,
and his paths beyond tracing out!

ROMANS 11:33

A person who says, "I know this horse," normally means not just "I have seen it before"; they mean, "I know how it behaves and can tell you how it ought to be handled." Such knowledge comes only through some prior acquaintance, seeing the horse in action, and trying to handle it oneself. In the case of human beings, the position is complicated by the fact that, unlike horses, people keep secrets. They do not show everybody all that is in their hearts. A few days are enough to get to know a horse as well as you will ever know it, but you may spend months and years doing this in company with another person and still have to say at the end of the time, "I don't really *know* him."

We recognize degrees in our knowledge of our fellow humans according to how much or how little they have opened up to us. "Knowing" God is of necessity a more complex business than "knowing" another person. If we spend the rest of our lives at it, there will still be more to comprehend. But the marvel of it is that God's riches are opened up to us to explore.

Journal: *What are some of the depths of God that you have begun to understand?*

Saturday/Sunday — *Royal Friend*

Let him who glories glory in this,
that he understands and knows me.

JEREMIAH 9:24 RSV

*I*magine that you are going to be introduced to someone whom you feel to be "above" you. (Think of meeting the prime minister of England.) If he confines himself to courteous formalities with you, you may be disappointed, but you do not feel able to complain. After all, you had no claim on his friendship. But if instead he starts at once to take you into his confidence and tells you frankly what is in his mind on matters of common concern, if he goes on to invite you to join him in particular undertakings he has planned and asks you to make yourself permanently available for this kind of collaboration whenever he needs you, then you feel enormously privileged. If life seemed unimportant and dreary hitherto, it takes on new brilliance.

This illustrates (dimly) what it means to know God. Well might God say through Jeremiah, "Let him who glories glory in this, that he understands and knows me," for knowing God is a relationship calculated to thrill a person's heart.

Pray: *In prayer, enter God's presence with all the respect due royalty—a King who has made you his friend.*

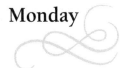

Monday

Piercing Truth

*I am a stranger on earth;
do not hide your commands from me.*

PSALM 119:19

$\mathcal{T}$he almighty Creator, the Lord of hosts, the great God before whom the nations are as a drop in a bucket, comes to you and begins to talk to you through the words and truths of holy Scripture. Perhaps you have been acquainted with the Bible and Christian truth for many years and it has meant little to you, but one day you wake up to the fact that God is actually speaking to you—you!—through the biblical message. As you listen to what God is saying, you find yourself brought low, for God talks to you about your sin, guilt, weakness, blindness, and folly, and he compels you to judge yourself hopeless and helpless and to cry out for forgiveness. When God reveals himself to us, he does not keep his desires hidden. Instead he does us the favor of showing us what he expects of his people.

Pray: *What is God showing you about your sin? Confess to him and enjoy the intimacy of forgiveness.*

Tuesday

Colaborers

We are God's fellow workers.

1 CORINTHIANS 3:9

*S*cripture leads to confession of sin and divine forgiveness. But this is not all. You come to realize, as you listen, that God is actually opening his heart to you, making friends with you, and enlisting you as a colleague (in Karl Barth's phrase, a "covenant partner"). It is a staggering thing, but it is true—the relationship in which sinful human beings know God is one in which God, so to speak, takes them onto his staff, to be henceforth his fellow workers and personal friends. From being Satan's prisoner, you find yourself transferred to a position of trust in the service of God. At once life is transformed.

Whether being a servant is a matter for shame or for pride depends on whose servant you are. Many have said what pride they felt in rendering personal service to Sir Winston Churchill during World War II. How much more should it be a matter of pride and glorying to know and serve the Lord of heaven and earth!

Reflect: *How are you participating in God's work on earth today?*

Wednesday   *God's Sheep*

> *My sheep listen to my voice;*
> *I know them, and they follow me.*
> *I give them eternal life, and they*
> *shall never perish; no one can*
> *snatch them out of my hand.*

JOHN 10:27-28

The Bible tells us that we know God in the manner of a son knowing his father, a wife knowing her husband, a subject knowing his king, and a sheep knowing its shepherd (these are the four main analogies employed). All four analogies point to a relation in which the knower "looks up" to the one known and in which the latter takes responsibility for the welfare of the former. This is part of the biblical concept of knowing God, that those who know him—that is, those by whom he allows himself to be known—are loved and cared for by him.

Pray: *Put yourself in the place of the sheep described in John 10:27-28. Slowly and prayerfully, read the passage, pausing to pray after each phrase.*

Thursday   *Other Sheep*

> *[Jesus said,] "I have other sheep that are not*
> *of this sheep pen. I must bring them also.*
> *They too will listen to my voice, and there*
> *shall be one flock and one shepherd. . . .*
> *I and the Father are one."*

JOHN 10:16, 30

*W*e should be clear in our minds as to what knowing Jesus Christ means. The disciples were ordinary Galileans with no special claims on the interest of Jesus. But Jesus—the rabbi who spoke with authority, the prophet who was more than a prophet, the master who evoked in them increasing awe and devotion till they could not but acknowledge him as their God—found them, called them to himself, took them into his confidence, and enrolled them as his agents to declare to the world the kingdom of God. And the sense of allegiance and privilege that this knowledge brought transformed their whole lives.

Now Jesus Christ is risen! One of the things this means is that the victim of Calvary is now loose and at large so that anyone anywhere can enjoy the same kind of relationship with him as the disciples had in the days of his flesh.

Reflect: *Enjoy your place as one of Jesus' "other sheep."*

Friday

Eternal Shepherd

The LORD is my shepherd,
I shall not be in want.

PSALM 23:1

*M*y sheep listen to my voice," says Jesus; "I know them, and they follow me" (John 10:27). "Come to me, all you who are weary and burdened, and I will give you rest. Take my yoke upon you and learn from me . . . and you will find rest" (Matthew 11:28-29). Jesus' voice is "heard" when Jesus' claim is acknowledged, his promise trusted, and his call answered. From then on, Jesus is known as shepherd, and those who trust him he knows as his own sheep. "I know them, and they follow me. I give them eternal life, and they shall never perish; no one can snatch them out of my hand" (John 10:27-28). To know Jesus is to be saved by Jesus, here and hereafter, from sin, guilt, and death.

Journal: *Picture yourself in the various biblical images above. Sketch your place in one of these scenes.*

Saturday/Sunday   *Personal Dealing*

> *Now this is eternal life: that they*
> *may know you, the only true God, and*
> *Jesus Christ, whom you have sent.*

JOHN 17:3

*K*nowing God is a matter of personal dealing, as is all direct acquaintance with personal beings. Knowing God is a matter of dealing with him as he opens up to you and of being dealt with by him as he takes knowledge of you. The width of our knowledge *about* him is no gauge of the depth of our knowledge *of* him. John Owen and John Calvin knew more theology than John Bunyan or Billy Bray, but who would deny that the latter pair knew their God every bit as well as the former? (All four, of course, were beavers for the Bible, which counts for far more anyway than a formal theological training.) A simple Bible reader and a sermon hearer who is full of the Holy Spirit will develop a far deeper acquaintance with his God and Savior than a more learned scholar who is content with being theologically correct. The reason is that the former will deal with God regarding the practical application of truth to his life, whereas the latter will not.

Reflect: *How open are you to "personal dealing" by God?*

Monday   *Tasting God*

Taste and see that the LORD is good.

PSALM 34:8

*K*nowing God is a matter of personal involvement—mind, will, and feeling. It would not be a fully personal relationship otherwise. To get to know another person, you have to commit yourself to his company and interests and be ready to identify yourself with his concerns. Without this, your relationship can only be superficial and flavorless. "Taste and see that the LORD is good," says the psalmist. We do not know another person's real quality till we have "tasted" the experience of friendship. Friends are, so to speak, communicating flavors to each other all the time by sharing their attitudes both toward each other (think of people in love) and toward everything else that is of common concern. As they open their hearts to each other by what they say and do, each "tastes" the quality of the other, for sorrow or for joy. This is an essential aspect of the knowledge that friends have of each other; and the same applies to the Christian's knowledge of God, which is itself a relationship between friends.

Journal: *God is good. How have you seen that in your involvement with him?*

Tuesday

Passion for God

When [Barnabas] arrived and saw the evidence of the grace of God, he was glad and encouraged them all to remain true to the Lord with all their hearts.

ACTS 11:23

*T*he emotional side of knowing God is often played down for fear of encouraging maudlin self-absorption. It is true that there is nothing more irreligious than self-absorbed religion, and it is constantly needful to stress that God does not exist for our comfort or happiness or satisfaction or to provide us with "religious experiences." But, for all of this, we must not lose sight of the fact that knowing God is an emotional relationship, as well as an intellectual and volitional one, and could not indeed be a deep relation between persons were it not so.

Believers rejoice when God is honored and vindicated, and they feel the acutest distress when they see God flouted. Christians know transports of delight as God brings home to them the glory of the everlasting love with which he has loved them. By contrast, the psalmist wrote, "streams of tears flow from my eyes, for your law is not obeyed" (Psalm 119:136). This is the emotional and experiential side of friendship with God.

Reflect: *What is your emotional involvement with God?*

Wednesday

Grace Came First

*You know God—or rather
are known by God . . .*

GALATIANS 4:9

*K*nowing God is a matter of grace. It is a relationship in which the initiative throughout is with God—as it must be, since God is so completely above us and we have so completely forfeited all claim on his favor by our sins. We do not make friends with *God;* *God* makes friends with *us*, bringing us to know him by making his love known to us.

Paul expresses this thought of the priority of grace in our knowledge of God when he writes to the Galatians, "Now that you know God—*or rather are known by God . . .* " What comes to the surface in this qualifying clause is the apostle's sense that grace came first, and remains fundamental, in his reader's salvation. Their knowing God was the consequence of God's taking knowledge of them. They know him by faith because he first singled them out by grace.

Reflect: *"Grace came first." How can you respond to the God who builds his relationship with you on that kind of start?*

Thursday

Listening to the Shepherd

Now I know in part; then I shall know fully, even as I am fully known.

1 CORINTHIANS 13:12

*T*he word *know* is a sovereign-grace word, pointing to God's initiative in loving, choosing, redeeming, calling, and preserving. That God is fully aware of us—"knowing us through and through," as we say—is certainly part of what is meant, as appears from the contrast between our imperfect knowledge of God and his perfect knowledge of us in 1 Corinthians 13:12. But it is not the main meaning. The main meaning comes out in passages like the following: "The LORD said to Moses, . . . 'I am pleased with you and *I know you by name*'" (Exodus 33:17). "Before I formed you [Jeremiah] in the womb *I knew you*" (Jeremiah 1:5). "My sheep listen to my voice; *I know them*" (John 10:27). Here God's knowledge of those who are his is associated with his whole purpose of saving mercy. It is a knowledge that implies personal affection, redeeming action, covenant faithfulness, and providential watchfulness toward those whom God knows. It implies, in other words, salvation now and forever.

Pray: *In prayer, pour out all that you are to the God who knows you.*

Friday

Humbling Friendship

*God made him [Jesus] who had no sin
to be sin for us, so that in him we might
become the righteousness of God.*

2 CORINTHIANS 5:21

There is, certainly, great cause for humility in the thought that God sees all the twisted things about me that my fellow humans do not see (and I am glad!) and that he sees more corruption in me than I see in myself (which, in all conscience, is enough). There is, however, equally great incentive to worship and love God in the thought that, for some unfathomable reason, he desires to be my friend and has given his Son to die for me in order to realize this purpose. We can hardly overvalue this gift: not only that we know God but that he knows us.

Journal: *Write a prayer of worship and love to God as a response to the friendship he has given to you.*

Saturday/Sunday

No Idols

You shall not make for yourself an idol.

EXODUS 20:4

*T*he purpose of the second commandment is plain. Negatively, it is a warning against ways of worship and religious practice that lead us to dishonor God and falsify his truth. Positively, it is a summons to recognize that God the Creator is transcendent, mysterious, and inscrutable, beyond the range of any imagining or philosophical guesswork of which we are capable. Hence it summons us to humble ourselves, to listen and learn of him, and to let him teach us what he is like and how we should think of him.

God is not the sort of person we are. His wisdom, his aims, his scale of value, and his mode of procedure differ so vastly from our own that we cannot possibly guess our way to them by intuition or infer them by analogy from our notion of ideal manhood. "My thoughts are not your thoughts," God tells us, "neither are your ways my ways," for "as the heavens are higher than the earth, so are my ways higher than your ways, and my thoughts than your thoughts" (Isaiah 55:8-9).

Reflect: *Reflect on the second commandment and your practice (or neglect) of obeying it.*

Monday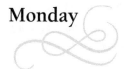

True Worship

*God is a spirit, and his worshipers
must worship in spirit and in truth.*

JOHN 4:24

Do we worship the one true God in truth? You may say, how can I tell? Well, the test is this. The God of the Bible has spoken through his Son. The light of the knowledge of his glory is given to us in the face of Jesus Christ. So do I look habitually to the person and work of the Lord Jesus Christ as showing me the final truth about the nature and the grace of God? Do I see all the purposes of God as centering on him? If I have been enabled to see this, and in mind and heart to go to Calvary and lay hold of the Calvary solution, then I can know that I truly worship the true God, that he is my God, and that I am even now enjoying eternal life, according to our Lord's own definition. "Now this is eternal life: that they may know you, the only true God, and Jesus Christ, whom you have sent" (John 17:3).

Reflect: *How well do your thoughts and actions meet these criteria of "spirit and truth" worship?*

Tuesday

Three in One

*May the grace of the Lord Jesus Christ,
and the love of God, and the fellowship
of the Holy Spirit be with you all.*

2 CORINTHIANS 13:14

It is often assumed that the doctrine of the Trinity, just because it is mysterious, is a piece of theological lumber that we can get on very happily without. Yet we sing of the Trinity in the doxology: "Glory be to the Father," sings the church, "and to the Son, and to the Holy Ghost." What is this, we ask: praise to three gods? No. Praise to one God in three persons. As the old hymn puts it,

> Jehovah! Father, Spirit, Son!
> Mysterious Godhead! Three in One!

This is the God Christians worship—the triune Jehovah. The heart of Christian faith in God is the revealed mystery of the Trinity.

Reflect: *When did you last encounter a sermon, talk, study, article, or book on the subject of the Trinity? If this has been rare in your Christian experience, what do you think you might be missing?*

Wednesday

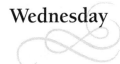

In the Beginning: God

There is but one God, the Father,
from whom all things came and for
whom we live; and there is but one Lord,
Jesus Christ, through whom all things
came and through whom we live.

1 CORINTHIANS 8:6

*I*n the opening sentences of his Gospel, John introduces us to the mystery of two distinct persons within the unity of the Godhead. This is the deep end of theology, no doubt, but John throws us straight into it. "In the beginning was the Word, and the Word was *with* God, and the Word *was* God" (John 1:1). The Word was a person in fellowship with God, and the Word was himself personally and eternally divine. He was, as John proceeds to tell us, the only Son of the Father. John sets this mystery of one God in two persons at the head of his Gospel because he knows that nobody can make heads or tails of the words and works of Jesus of Nazareth till he has grasped the fact that this Jesus is in truth God the Son.

Journal: *"Jesus is in truth God the Son." Read three chapters of any one of the four Gospels. Jot down what this section of Scripture reveals of Jesus' nature and character. What do your findings reveal about the being of God?*

Thursday

Comforter

*I will pray the Father, and he shall
give you another Comforter, that
he may abide with you for ever.*

JOHN 14:16 KJV

In John's account of our Lord's last talk to his disciples, he reports how the Savior, having explained that he was going to prepare a place for them in his Father's house, went on to promise them the gift of "another Comforter." The thoughts of encouragement, support, assistance, care, and the shouldering of responsibility for another's welfare are all conveyed by this word *Comforter.*

Another Comforter—yes, because Jesus was their original Comforter, and the newcomer's task was to continue this side of his ministry. It follows, therefore, that we can only appreciate all that our Lord meant when he spoke of "another Comforter" as we look back over all that he himself had done in the way of love, care, patient instruction, and provision for the disciples' well-being during his own three years of personal ministry to them. "He will care for you," Christ was saying in effect, "in the way that I have cared for you." Truly a remarkable person!

Reflect: *Reflect on the Holy Spirit as Comforter. How has he been this to you, perhaps even when you were not aware? Thank him.*

Friday

Word and Breath

By the word of the LORD were
the heavens made, their starry host
by the breath of his mouth.

PSALM 33:6

The new Comforter is "the Spirit of truth," "the Holy Spirit" (John 14:17, 26). This name denoted deity. In the Old Testament, God's *word* and God's *Spirit* are parallel figures. God's word is his almighty speech; God's Spirit is his almighty breath. Both phrases convey the thought of his power in action. The speech and the breath of God appear together in the record of creation. John told us in the prologue that the divine Word spoken of here is a person. Our Lord later gives parallel teaching to the effect that the divine Spirit is also a person. And he confirms his witness to the deity of this personal Spirit by calling him the *Holy* Spirit, as later he was to speak of the *Holy* Father (John 17:11).

Reflect: *Meditate on Jesus as God's Word and the Holy Spirit as God's breath. After a time of thoughtful silence, use your own words and breath to praise God.*

Saturday/Sunday

God's Will

*[Jesus said,] The Spirit of truth,
which proceedeth from the
Father, he shall testify of me.*

JOHN 15:26 KJV

John's Gospel shows how Christ related the Spirit's mission to the will and purpose of the Father and the Son. Having sent the eternal Son into the world, the Father now recalls him to glory and sends the Spirit to take his place. Thus John records our Lord's disclosure of the mystery of the Trinity: three persons and one God, the Son doing the will of the Father, and the Spirit doing the will of the Father and the Son. And the point stressed is that the Spirit, who comes to Christ's disciples "to be with you forever" (John 14:16), is coming to exercise the ministry of a comforter in Christ's stead. If, therefore, the ministry of Christ the Comforter was important, the ministry of the Holy Spirit the Comforter can scarcely be less important. If the work that Christ did matters to the church, the work that the Spirit does must matter also.

Reflect: *Reflect on the interconnections of God's will between the three persons of the Trinity as described above. How might this discernment shape your own participation in God's work?*

Monday   *Witnesses*

> *You will be my witnesses . . .*
> *to the ends of the earth.*

ACTS 1:8

*W*hen Christ left the world, he committed his cause to his disciples. He made them responsible for going and making disciples in all the nations. Such was their appointed task.

But what sort of witnesses were they likely to prove? They had never been good pupils. They had consistently failed to understand Christ and missed the point of his teaching throughout his earthly ministry. How could they be expected to do better now that he had gone? Was it not virtually certain that, with the best will in the world, they would soon get the truth of the gospel inextricably mixed up with a mass of well-meant misconceptions, and their witness would rapidly be reduced to a twisted, garbled, hopeless muddle?

The answer to this question is no, because Christ sent the Holy Spirit to teach them all truth and so save them from all error. The Spirit would remind them of what they had been taught already and reveal to them the rest of what their Lord meant them to learn.

Reflect: *What is your role in the task of a witness? How might the Holy Spirit assist you in that work?*

Tuesday

Spirit Inspired

[Jesus said,] "The Spirit will take from what is mine and make it known to you."

JOHN 16:15

The promise was that, taught by the Spirit, the original disciples should be enabled to speak as so many mouths of Christ. Just as the Old Testament prophets had been able to introduce their sermons with the words "Thus saith the Lord Jehovah," so the New Testament apostles might with equal truth be able to say of their teaching, oral or written, "Thus saith the Lord Jesus Christ."

And the thing happened. The Spirit came to the disciples and testified to them of Christ and his salvation, according to the promise. Paul writes, "God has revealed it to us by his Spirit. . . . We have . . . received . . . the Spirit who is from God, that we may understand what God has freely given us" (1 Corinthians 2:10-12).

The Spirit testified to the apostles by revealing to them all truth and inspiring them to communicate it with all truthfulness. Hence the gospel. And hence the New Testament. But the world would have had neither without the Holy Spirit.

Reflect: *Read one of the short letters of the New Testament. Thank God the Holy Spirit for what you find there.*

Wednesday

Holy Vision

*[The Holy Spirit] will convince
the world concerning sin and
righteousness and judgment.*

JOHN 16:8 RSV

*W*ithout the Spirit, there would be no faith and no new birth—in short, no Christians. The blind do not respond to the stimulus of light. What follows, then? Should we conclude that preaching the gospel is a waste of time and write off evangelism as a hopeless enterprise, foredoomed to fail? No, because the Spirit abides with the church to testify of Christ. To the apostles, he testified by revealing and inspiring. To the rest of us, down the ages, he testifies by illuminating: opening blinded eyes, restoring spiritual vision, enabling sinners to see that the gospel is indeed God's truth, Scripture is indeed God's Word, and Christ is indeed God's Son. "When he comes," our Lord promised, "he will convince the world concerning sin and righteousness and judgment."

Reflect: *When has God's Spirit opened your eyes? What did he reveal to you about yourself? about God? Pray now for the Spirit's illuminating power in someone who needs to know God. Pray also for the Holy Spirit to reveal the role he has for you in the life of that person.*

Thursday

Convincing Spirit

My speech and my message were not in plausible words of wisdom, but in demonstration of the Spirit and of power, that your faith might not rest in the wisdom of men but in the power of God.

1 CORINTHIANS 2:4-5 RSV

*W*ithout the Spirit we could not believe. It is not for us to imagine that we can prove the truth of Christianity by our own arguments. Nobody can prove the truth of Christianity except the Holy Spirit, by his own almighty work of renewing the blinded heart.

It is the sovereign prerogative of Christ's Spirit to convince men's consciences of the truth of Christ's gospel. Christ's human witnesses must learn to ground their hopes of success not on clever presentation of the truth by man but on powerful demonstration of the truth by the Spirit. Paul points the way here: "When I came to you, brethren, I did not come proclaiming to you the testimony of God in lofty words or wisdom" (1 Corinthians 2:1 RSV).

Because the Spirit does bear witness in this way, people come to faith when the gospel is preached. But without the Spirit, there would not be a Christian in the world.

Pray: *Thank God for the work of his Spirit in convincing you.*

Friday

Lamp Light

*Your word is a lamp to my feet
and a light for my path.*

PSALM 119:105

Do we honor the Holy Spirit by recognizing and relying on his work? Or do we slight him by ignoring it and thereby dishonoring not merely the Spirit but also the Lord who sent him?

In our faith: Do we acknowledge the authority of the Bible, the prophetic Old Testament, and the apostolic New Testament that he inspired? Do we read and hear it with the reverence and receptiveness that are due to the Word of God? If not, we dishonor the Holy Spirit.

In our life: Do we apply the authority of the Bible and live by the Bible, whatever anyone may say against it, recognizing that God's Word cannot but be true and that what God has said he certainly means and will stand behind? If not, we dishonor the Holy Spirit who gave us the Bible.

Reflect: *In the presence of God's Spirit, prayerfully examine your conscience using the questions above. Page through your Bible. Does it bear the marks of frequent use? Reflect on the events of your past week. How have you lived (and not lived) by the teachings of Scripture? Pray about your findings.*

Saturday/Sunday

Honoring the Spirit

> *He who has an ear, let him hear*
> *what the Spirit says to the churches.*

REVELATION 2:7

*D*o we honor the Spirit in our witness? Do we remember that the Holy Spirit alone, by his witness, can authenticate our witness? And do we look to him to do so and trust him to do so? Do we show the reality of our trust, as Paul did, by eschewing the gimmicks of human cleverness? If not, we dishonor the Holy Spirit.

Can we doubt that the present barrenness of the church's life is God's judgment on us for the way in which we have dishonored the Holy Spirit? And, in that case, what hope have we of relief from emptiness till we learn in our thinking and our praying and our practice to honor the Holy Spirit? "He will testify . . ." (John 15:26).

Journal: *How does your church honor the Holy Spirit in thinking, praying, and practice? How do you personally practice this kind of honor? Journal some ways that this is already taking place. Outline one way that your church could better honor the Holy Spirit. Consider how and to whom you can make this suggestion.*

Monday   *Open Our Eyes*

> *Open my eyes that I may see*
> *wonderful things in your law.*

PSALM 119:18

*W*e sometimes feel that we are mere spectators of the Bible world, and that is all. Our unspoken thought is, *Yes, God did all that then, and very wonderful it was for the people involved, but how does it touch us now? We don't live in the same world. How can the record of God's words and deeds in Bible times, the record of his dealings with Abraham and Moses and David and the rest, help us who have to live in the age of technology?* We cannot see how the two worlds link up, and hence again and again we find ourselves feeling that the things we read about in the Bible can have no application for us. And when, as is so often true, these things are in themselves thrilling and glorious, we have a sense of being excluded from them.

Most Bible readers have known this feeling. In these moments we need to express our desire for understanding to God.

Journal: *When and how have you known some of the feelings described above? What have you gained by the Scripture's setting in a world so different from your own? How have you continued your search for finding God through Scripture?*

Tuesday

Immutable God

I the LORD do not change.

MALACHI 3:6

*H*ow can our sense of remoteness from the biblical experience of God be overcome? Many things might be said, but the crucial point is seeing the link between our situation and that of the various Bible characters in the wrong place. It is true that, in terms of space, time, and culture, they and the historical epoch to which they belonged are a long way from us. But the link between them and us is not found at that level. *The link is God himself.* For the God with whom they had to do is the same God with whom we have to do. We could sharpen the point by saying he is *exactly* the same God, for God does not change in the least particular. Thus it appears that the truth on which we must dwell, in order to dispel the feeling that there is an unbridgeable gulf between the position of men and women in Bible times and in our own, is the truth of God's immutability.

Reflect: *Bring to mind a favorite character from Scripture. In light of God's immutability, what links do you find with this person?*

Wednesday

Changeless Life

*From everlasting to
everlasting you are God.*

PSALM 90:2

*C*reated things have a beginning and an ending, but not so their Creator. The answer to the child's question, "Who made God?" is simply that God did not need to be made, for he was always there. He exists forever, and he is always the same. He does not grow older. His life does not wax or wane. He does not gain new powers nor lose those that he once had. He does not mature or develop. He does not get stronger, weaker, or wiser as time goes by. "He cannot change for the better," wrote A. W. Pink, "for he is already perfect; and being perfect, he cannot change for the worse."

The first and fundamental difference between the Creator and his creatures is that they are mutable and their nature admits of change, whereas God is immutable and can never cease to be what he is. As the old hymn puts it,

We blossom and flourish as leaves on the tree,
And wither and perish—but naught changeth Thee.

Pray: *Read all of Psalm 90, stopping now and then to meditate and pray on what you find there.*

Thursday

Changeless Character

Every good endowment and every perfect gift is from above, coming down from the Father of lights with whom there is no variation or shadow due to change.

JAMES 1:17 RSV

Strain, shock, or a lobotomy can alter the character of a person, but nothing can alter the character of God. In the course of a human life, a kind, equable person may turn bitter and crotchety. A person of goodwill may grow cynical and callous. But nothing of this sort happens to the Creator. He never becomes less truthful, merciful, just, or good than he used to be.

The character of God is today, and always will be, exactly what it was in Bible times. So James, in a passage that deals with God's goodness and holiness, his generosity to us, and his hostility to sin, speaks of God as one who never falters. This is a great comfort to us as we live in a world that is ever changing and failing us in every way. God's character will always be exactly as it is.

Journal: *Write a letter to God thanking him for his consistent character.*

Friday

Changeless Name

God said to Moses, "I AM WHO I AM."

EXODUS 3:14

*I*n Exodus 3 God announced his name to Moses as "I AM WHO I AM." This name is not a description of God but simply a declaration of his self-existence and his eternal changelessness. It is a reminder to humankind that he has life in himself and that what he is now, he is eternally.

In Exodus 34 we read how God proclaimed his name, "the LORD," to Moses by listing the various facets of his holy character: "abounding in love and faithfulness, maintaining love to thousands, and forgiving wickedness, rebellion and sin" (verse 6). This proclamation supplements that of Exodus 3 by telling us what in fact Yahweh is. The proclamation of Exodus 3 supplements this by telling us that God is forever what he told Moses he was three thousand years ago.

God's moral character is changeless.

Reflect: *If a person were to say, "I am who I am," we would think that person belligerent. Why is this name for God a comfort?*

Saturday/Sunday   *Changeless Truth*

> *The grass withers . . . but the word*
> *of our God will stand for ever.*

> **ISAIAH 40:8 RSV**

*P*eople sometimes say things they do not really mean simply because they do not know their own minds. All of us sometimes have to take back our words because they have ceased to express what we think. Sometimes we have to eat our words because hard facts refute them.

The words of human beings are unstable things. But not so the words of God. They stand forever as abidingly valid expressions of his mind and thought. No circumstances prompt him to recall them. No changes in his own thinking require him to amend them.

When we read our Bibles, therefore, we need to remember that God still stands behind all the promises, demands, statements of purpose, and words of warning that are there addressed to New Testament believers. These are not relics of a bygone age but an eternally valid revelation of the mind of God toward his people in all generations, so long as this world lasts. Nothing can annul God's eternal truth.

Journal: *"Nothing can annul God's eternal truth." Journal your response to this statement.*

Monday

Changeless Ways

As for God, his way is perfect.

2 SAMUEL 22:31

*G*od's ways do not change. Still he blesses those on whom he sets his love in a way that humbles them so that all the glory may be his alone. Still he hates the sins of his people and uses all kinds of inward and outward pains and griefs to wean their hearts from compromise and disobedience. Still he seeks the fellowship of his people and sends them both sorrows and joys in order to detach their love from other things and attach it to himself. Still he teaches believers to value his promised gifts by making them wait for those gifts, and compelling them to pray persistently for them, before he bestows them.

So we read of God dealing with his people in the Scripture record, and so he deals with them still. His aims and principles of action remain consistent. He does not at any time act out of character. Our ways, we know, are pathetically inconstant—but not God's.

Pray: *Prayerfully reread the paragraphs above, pausing after each sentence to thank God for specific instances in which you have seen his ways at work.*

Tuesday

Changeless Purposes

The plans of the LORD stand firm forever.

PSALM 33:11

*G*od's purposes do not change. His plans are made on the basis of a complete knowledge and control that extends to all things, past, present, and future, so that there can be no sudden emergencies or unexpected developments to take him by surprise. What God does in time, he planned from eternity. All that he planned in eternity, he carries out in time. And all that he has in his Word committed himself to do will infallibly be done.

It is true that a group of texts speak of God as repenting (Genesis 6:6-7; 1 Samuel 15:11; 2 Samuel 24:16; Joel 2:13-14; Jonah 3:10). The reference in each case is to a reversal of God's previous treatment of particular people, consequent upon their reaction to that treatment. But there is no suggestion that this reaction was not foreseen or that it took God by surprise. No change in his eternal purpose is implied when he begins to deal with a person in a new way.

God's announced intentions do not change. No part of his eternal plan changes.

Reflect: *Reflect on various expressions of time and eternity in the paragraphs above. Praise God for what you find there.*

Wednesday

Changeless Christ

*Jesus Christ is the same
yesterday and today and forever.*

HEBREWS 13:8

*G*od's Son does not change. His touch has still its ancient power. Where is the sense of distance and difference between believers in Bible times and ourselves? It is excluded. On what grounds? On the grounds that God does not change. Fellowship with him, trust in his Word, living by faith, standing on the promises of God—these are essentially the same realities for us today as they were for Old and New Testament believers.

This thought brings comfort as we enter into the perplexities of each day. Amid all the changes and uncertainties of life in a nuclear age, God and his Christ remain the same—almighty to save.

But the thought brings a searching challenge too. If our God is the same as the God of New Testament believers, then our Christian conduct and witness should rise to the same level as theirs.

Reflect: *If Jesus Christ is without change, how does this affect your relationship with him?*

Thursday   *Majesty*

*The LORD reigns, he is robed in
majesty. . . . Your throne was established
long ago; you are from all eternity.*

PSALM 93:1-2

*O*ur word *majesty* comes from Latin; it means "greatness."
When we ascribe majesty to someone, we are acknowledging
greatness in that person and voicing our respect for it, as for instance when we speak of "Her Majesty" the queen.

The word *majesty,* when applied to God, is always a declaration of his greatness and an invitation to worship. The same is
true when the Bible speaks of God as being "on high" and "in
heaven." The thought here is not that God is far distant from us
in space but that he is far above us in greatness and therefore is
to be adored.

People today, though they cherish great thoughts of themselves, have as a rule small thoughts of God. If we restore majesty
in all its meaning to our vocabulary for God, our worship will be
invigorated, and our understanding of God will be expanded.

Pray: *Spend several minutes meditating on God's majesty. Then
pray in a manner appropriate for majesty.*

Friday

God Is Great

The LORD is the great God,
the great King. . . . Come, let us
bow down in worship.

PSALM 95:3, 6

A well-known book is called *Your God Is Too Small*. It is a timely title.

We are poles apart from our evangelical forefathers at this point. When you start reading Luther or Edwards or Whitefield, though your doctrine may be theirs, you soon find yourself wondering whether you have any acquaintance at all with the mighty God whom they knew so intimately.

Today, vast stress is laid on the thought that God is personal, but this truth is so stated as to leave the impression that God is a person of the same sort as we are—weak, inadequate, ineffective, a little pathetic. But this is not the God of the Bible!

Our personal life is a finite thing: it is limited in every direction, in space, in time, in knowledge, in power. But God is not so limited. He is eternal, infinite, and almighty. He has us in his hands; we never have him in ours. Like us, he is personal. But unlike us, he is *great*. The Bible never lets us lose sight of his majesty and his unlimited dominion over all his creatures.

Journal: *"[God] has us in his hands; we never have him in ours." Journal the implications of this statement.*

Saturday/Sunday   *God Is Personal*

> *The man and his wife heard the sound of the*
> *LORD God as he was walking in the garden in*
> *the cool of the day, and they hid from the*
> *LORD. . . . But the LORD God called to the man,*
> *"Where are you?"*

GENESIS 3:8-9

*R*ight from the start, the Bible's story is told in such a way as to impress on us the twin truths that the God to whom we are being introduced is both *personal* and *majestic*. Genesis reveals the personal nature of God expressed in vivid terms. He deliberates with himself, saying, "Let us . . ." (Genesis 1:26). He brings the animals to Adam to see what Adam will call them (2:19). He walks in the garden calling to Adam (3:8-9). He asks people questions (4:9). He comes down from heaven in order to find out what his creatures are doing (11:5). He is so grieved by human wickedness that he repents of making them (6:6-7). Representations of God like these show us that God is not a mere cosmic principle, impersonal and indifferent. Rather, he is a living Person, thinking, feeling, active, approving of good, disapproving of evil, interested in his creatures all the time.

Reflect: *Reflect on the fact that the same God who is majestic is also personal. Bare your soul to him in prayer.*

SPRING

Monday

El Shaddai

Is anything too hard for the LORD?

GENESIS 18:14

*G*enesis sets before us a presentation of God's greatness no less vivid than his personality. The God of Genesis is the Creator, bringing order out of chaos, calling life into being by his word, making Adam from earth's dust and Eve from Adam's rib (chapters 1-2). And he is Lord of all that he has made. Hagar did well to name him El Roi, "The God who sees me," and call her son Ishmael, "God hears," for God does in truth both hear and see, and nothing escapes him. His own name for himself is El Shaddai, "God Almighty," and all his actions illustrate the omnipotence that his name proclaims. Proof of this is given by his detailed predictions of the tremendous destiny that he purposed to work out for Abraham's seed (12:1-3 and so on). Such, in brief, is the majesty of God according to the first chapters of Genesis.

Pray: *Meditate on "El Shaddai" as a name for God. In prayer, respond to this quality of God's nature.*

Tuesday

All-Knowing

*O LORD, you have searched
me and you know me.*

PSALM 139:1

*T*here are no limits to God's knowledge of me. Just as I am never left alone, so I never go unnoticed. "O LORD, you have searched me and you know me. You know when I sit and when I rise [all my actions and movements]; you perceive my thoughts [all that goes on in my mind] from afar. . . . You are familiar with all my ways [all my habits, plans, aims, desires, as well as all my life to date]. Before a word is on my tongue [spoken or meditated] you know it completely, O LORD" (Psalm 139:1-4).

I can hide my heart and my past and my plans for the future from those around me, but I cannot hide anything from God. I can talk in a way that deceives my fellow creatures as to what I really am, but nothing I say or do can deceive God. He sees through all my reserve and pretense. He knows me as I really am—better, indeed, than I know myself.

Journal: *Carefully study Psalm 139:1-6. How do you feel about God knowing you this intensely? Journal your response as a prayer to him.*

Wednesday   *Always There*

Where can I go from your Spirit?

PSALM 139:7

*H*ow may we form a right idea of God's greatness? We begin by removing from our thoughts of God any limits that would make him small.

For an example of what the first step involves, look at Psalm 139, where the psalmist meditates on the infinite and unlimited nature of God's presence, knowledge, and power in relation to people. We are always in God's presence, he says. You can cut yourself off from your fellow human beings, but you cannot get away from your Creator. "You hem me in—behind and before. . . . Where can I go from your Spirit? Where can I flee from your presence? If I go up to the heavens [the sky], you are there; if I make my bed in the depths [the underworld], you are there. If I rise on the wings of the dawn, if I settle on the far side of the sea," I still cannot escape from the presence of God: "even there your hand will guide me" (verses 5-10). Nor can darkness, which hides me from human sight, shield me from God's gaze (verses 11-12).

Reflect: *Prayerfully read Psalm 139:7-12, reflecting on God's constant presence in your own life. Pray your response to that kind of care.*

Thursday

Wonderfully Made

I praise you because I am
fearfully and wonderfully made;
your works are wonderful.

PSALM 139:14

I could evade a small and trivial deity, but the true God is great and terrible just because he is always with me and his eye is always on me. Living becomes an awesome business when you realize that you spend every moment of your life in the sight and company of an omniscient, omnipresent Creator.

Nor is this all. The all-seeing God is also God Almighty, the resources of whose power are already revealed to me by the amazing complexity of my own physical body, which he made for me. Confronted with this, the psalmist's meditations turn to worship. "I praise you because I am fearfully and wonderfully made; your works are wonderful."

Here, then, is the first step in apprehending the greatness of God: to realize how unlimited are his wisdom, his presence, and his power.

Pray: *Consider the complexity of your own body, which began with two microscopic cells. God knew you even then—and loved you. Pray your response, committing your body (the good and not so good) to him.*

Friday

God's Hands

*Who has measured the [earth's]
waters in the hollow of his hand?*

ISAIAH 40:12

To know God's greatness, look at Isaiah 40. Here God speaks to people whose mood is the mood of many Christians today. We are despondent people, cowed people, secretly despairing people. We are people against whom the tide of events has been running for a long time. We are people who have ceased to believe that the cause of Christ can ever prosper again. Now see how God, through his prophet, reasons with such people.

Look at the tasks I have done, he says. Could you do them? Could any man do them? "Who has measured the waters in the hollow of his hand, or with the breadth of his hand marked off the heavens? Who has held the dust of the earth in a basket, or weighed the mountains on the scales and the hills in a balance?" (verse 12). Are you wise enough and mighty enough to do things like that? But I am, or I could not have made this world at all.

Behold your God!

Reflect: *Meditate on each phrase of Isaiah 40:12, trying to capture the immensity of each visual image. Use those pictures of greatness to "behold your God." Respond in worship.*

Saturday/Sunday   *Greater Than Nations*

*Surely the nations are like
a drop in a bucket.*

ISAIAH 40:15

*T*o know God's greatness, says the prophet Isaiah, look at the great national powers, at whose mercy you feel yourselves to be: Assyria, Egypt, Babylon. You stand in awe of them and feel afraid of them, so vastly do their armies and resources exceed yours. But now consider how God stands related to those mighty forces that you fear so much. "Surely the nations are like a drop in a bucket; they are regarded as dust on the scales. . . . Before [God] all the nations are as nothing; they are regarded by him as worthless and less than nothing" (Isaiah 40:15, 17). You tremble before the nations because you are much weaker than they. But God is so much greater than the nations that they are as nothing to him.

Behold your God!

Pray: *Read through the world news, focusing on nations in need or nations posing a threat to the cause of Christ. Pray for specific nations that God, whose greatness is far beyond all nations, will intervene, bringing justice, mercy, and peace.*

Monday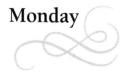

Greater Than the World

He sits enthroned above the
circle of the earth, and its people
are like grasshoppers.

Isaiah 40:22

To know God's greatness, look at the world. Consider the size of it, the variety and complexity of it. Think of the seven billion people who populate it and of the vast sky above it. What puny figures you and I are by comparison with the whole planet on which we live!

Yet what is this entire mighty planet by comparison with God? "He stretches out the heavens like a canopy, and spreads them out like a tent to live in" (Isaiah 40:22). The world dwarfs us all, but God dwarfs the world. The world is his footstool, above which he sits secure. He is greater than the world and all that is in it, so all the feverish activity of its bustling millions does no more to affect him than the chirping and jumping of grasshoppers in the summer sun.

Behold your God!

Reflect: *Study a world map or globe. Survey the various land-masses, noting mountains, cities, oceans. Reflect on the people there—those who do and those who do not know Christ. Pray for the world, recognizing that God's greatness far surpasses anything here.*

Tuesday

Greater Than the Greats

He brings princes to naught and reduces the rulers of this world to nothing.

ISAIAH 40:23

To know God's greatness, look at the world's great ones—the governors whose laws and policies determine the welfare of millions. Look at the would-be world rulers, the dictators and empire builders, who have it in their power to plunge the globe into war. Think of Sennacherib and Nebuchadnezzar. Think of Alexander, Napoleon, Hitler. Think of current heads of state, both good and evil.

Do you suppose that it is really these top men and women who determine which way the world will go? Think again, for God is greater than the world's great ones. "He brings princes to naught and reduces the rulers of this world to nothing." He is, as the Anglican prayer book says, "the only ruler of princes."

Behold your God!

Pray: *Select two heads of state: one apparently benevolent, the other reputed to be cruel. Pray for each, recognizing that if you could put all of the rulers of the world into one room, God would be greater than them all.*

Wednesday

Greater Than Stars

*Lift your eyes and look to
the heavens: Who created all these?
He who brings out the starry host one
by one, and calls them each by name.*

ISAIAH 40:26

To know God's greatness, look at the stars. The most universally awesome experience that humankind knows is to stand alone on a clear night and look at the stars. Nothing gives a greater sense of remoteness and distance. Nothing makes one feel more strongly one's own littleness and insignificance. Even beyond our sight hover millions of stars, billions of light-years in distance. Our minds reel. Our imaginations cannot grasp it. When we try to conceive of the unfathomable depths of outer space, we are left mentally numb and dizzy.

But what is this to God? "Because of his great power and mighty strength, not one [star] is missing" (Isaiah 40:26). It is God who brings out the stars. It was God who first set them in space. He is their Maker and Master—they are all in his hands and subject to his will. Such are his power and his majesty.

Behold your God!

Journal: *On the next starry night, go outside with your journal and a flashlight. Stretch out flat with your face to the heavens. Alternately think, pray, and write.*

Thursday

God Thoughts

> *"To whom will you compare me?*
> *Or who is my equal?" says the Holy One.*

ISAIAH 40:25

*I*saiah closes chapter 40 with three questions in God's name. The first is "To whom will you compare me?" This question rebukes wrong thoughts about God.

"Your thoughts of God are too human," said Luther to Erasmus. This is where most of us go astray. Our thoughts of God are not great enough. We fail to reckon with the reality of his limitless wisdom and power. Because we ourselves are limited and weak, we imagine that at some points God is too, and we find it hard to believe that he is not.

We think of God as too much like what we are. Put this mistake right, says God. Learn to acknowledge the full majesty of your incomparable God and Savior.

Journal: *"Your thoughts of God are too human," said Luther. Create a page of ways that God is beyond the human. Use this page as a step into worshipful prayer.*

Friday

No Complaints

Why do you say, O Jacob,
and complain, O Israel,
"My way is hidden from the LORD"?

ISAIAH 40:27

/saiah's second question in chapter 40 is "Why do you say, O Jacob, . . . 'My way is hidden from the LORD; my cause is disregarded by my God'?" (Isaiah 40:27). This question rebukes wrong thoughts about ourselves.

God has not abandoned us any more than he abandoned Job. He never abandons anyone on whom he has set his love. Nor does Christ, the good shepherd, ever lose track of his sheep. It is as false as it is irreverent to accuse God of forgetting, overlooking, or losing interest in the state and needs of his own people.

If you have been resigning yourself to the thought that God has left you high and dry, seek grace to be ashamed of yourself. Such unbelieving pessimism deeply dishonors our great God and Savior.

Reflect: *Consider whether your complaints are dishonoring to God, ignoring his greatness. Ask his grace to be honest with yourself and with him on this. Ask his help in drawing you to trust his love for you.*

Saturday/Sunday   *Hearing and Knowing*

Do you not know? Have you not heard?
The LORD is the everlasting God,
the Creator of the ends of the earth.
He will not grow tired or weary, and
his understanding no one can fathom.

ISAIAH 40:28

*I*saiah's third question in chapter 40 is "Hast thou not known? hast thou not heard, that the everlasting God, the LORD, the Creator of the ends of the earth, fainteth not, neither is weary?" (Isaiah 40:28 KJV). This question rebukes our slowness to believe in God's majesty.

God would save us out of our unbelief. "What is the trouble?" he asks. "Have you been imagining that I, the Creator, have grown old and tired? Has nobody ever told you the truth about Me?"

The rebuke is well deserved by many of us. How slow we are to believe in God *as God,* sovereign, all-seeing, and almighty. How little we make of the majesty of our Lord and Savior Christ! The need for us is to "wait upon the LORD" (Isaiah 40:31 KJV) in meditations on his majesty till we find our strength renewed through the writing of these things on our hearts.

Reflect: *Read and enjoy each phrase of Isaiah 40:28-31. Thank God for the hope you find there.*

Monday

Pagan Propitiation

*[Christ] is the propitiation for our sins:
and not for ours only, but also for
the sins of the whole world.*

1 JOHN 2:2 KJV

*P*rince Paris had carried off Princess Helen of Troy. The Greek expeditionary force had taken ships to recover her but was held up halfway by persistent contrary winds. Agamemnon, the Greek general, sent home for his daughter and ceremonially slaughtered her as a sacrifice to mollify the evidently hostile gods. The move paid off. West winds blew again, and the fleet reached Troy without further difficulty. This bit of the Trojan War legend, which dates from about 1000 BC, mirrors an idea of propitiation on which pagan religion all over the world, and in every age, has been built.

The Bible condemns paganism out of hand as a monstrous distortion of truth. One might expect, therefore, that there would be no place for the idea of propitiation in biblical religion. But we do not find this at all; just the opposite. The idea of propitiation —that is, of averting God's anger by an offering—runs right through the Bible.

Reflect: *What questions come to your mind regarding God's form of propitiation?*

Tuesday

Speaking the Truth

If we or an angel from heaven should preach a gospel other than the one we preached to you, let him be eternally condemned!

GALATIANS 1:8

*D*oes the word *propitiation* have any place in Christianity? In the faith of the New Testament, it is central: the love of God, the taking of human form by the Son, the meaning of the cross, Christ's heavenly intercession, the way of salvation—all are to be explained in terms of it. Any explanation from which the thought of propitiation is missing will be incomplete, and indeed actually misleading, by New Testament standards.

In saying this, we swim against a prevalent stream of false teaching. But we cannot help that. Paul wrote, "Even if we or an angel from heaven"—let alone a minister, bishop, college lecturer, university professor, or noted author—"should preach a gospel other than the one we preached to you, let him be eternally condemned!" (Galatians 1:8). And a gospel without propitiation at its heart is another gospel than that which Paul preached. The implications of this must not be evaded.

Reflect: *In what ways do you see propitiation as the true heart of the gospel?*

Wednesday

Human Need

*The wrath of God is being
revealed from heaven against all the
godlessness and wickedness of men.*

ROMANS 1:18

In the opening chapters of Romans, Paul paints a grim picture of human need. In Romans 1:18 Paul sets the stage for his declaration of the gospel by affirming that "the wrath of God is being revealed from heaven against all the godlessness and wickedness of men." In the rest of Romans 1 Paul traces out the present activity of God's wrath in the judicial hardening of apostate hearts, expressed in the thrice-repeated phrase "God gave them up" (see verses 24, 26, 28 KJV). Then in Romans 2:1-16 Paul confronts us with the certainty of the "day of wrath and revelation of the righteous judgment of God; who will render to every man according to his works: . . . unto them that . . . obey not the truth, but obey unrighteousness, shall be wrath and indignation . . . in the day when God shall judge the secrets of men, according to my gospel, by Jesus Christ" (verses 5-6, 8, 16 RV). Clearly humankind needs divine intervention.

Reflect: *Read Romans 1:1–2:16. What do you see here that shows human need for divine intervention?*

Thursday

God's Anger

Be holy, because I am holy.

LEVITICUS 11:44

What manner of thing is the wrath of God that was propitiated at Calvary? It is not the capricious, arbitrary, bad-tempered, and conceited anger that pagans attribute to their gods. It is not the sinful, resentful, malicious, infantile anger that we find among humans. It is a function of the holiness that is expressed in the demands of God's moral law ("Be holy, because I am holy").

His is righteous anger—the right reaction of moral perfection in the Creator toward moral perversity in the creature. Far from the manifestation of God's wrath in punishing sin being morally doubtful, the thing that would be morally doubtful would be for him not to show his wrath in this way. God is not just—that is, he does not act in the way that is right, he does not do what is proper to a judge—unless he inflicts on all sin and wrongdoing the penalty it deserves. God's anger leads to propitiation.

Reflect: *"God's anger leads to propitiation." What does this mean to humanity? to you? What does it suggest of the nature of God?*

Friday

God's Doing

It is by grace you have been saved,
through faith—and this is not from yourselves.

*I*n paganism the subjects propitiate their gods, and religion becomes a form of commercialism and indeed of bribery. In Christianity, however, God propitiates his wrath by his own action.

"God hath set forth [Christ Jesus]," says Paul, "to be a propitiation" (Romans 3:25 KJV). "He sent his Son," says John, "to be the propitiation for our sins" (1 John 4:10 KJV). The Bible insists that it was God himself who took the initiative in quenching his own wrath against those whom, despite their ill desert, he loved and had chosen to save.

How does this take place? "By grace" (Ephesians 2:8). And of course grace is mercy contrary to merit. It is love for the unlovely and unlovable.

By what means does grace operate? "Through the redemption that is in Christ Jesus" (Romans 3:24 KJV). Redemption is rescue by ransom.

How is it that, to those who put faith in him, Christ Jesus is the source, means, and substance of redemption? Because, says Paul, God set him forth to be a propitiation. From this divine initiative the reality and availability of redemption flow.

Journal: *Write a prayer of thanks for "God's doing" of propitiation.*

- 105 -

Saturday/Sunday

Love One Another

This is how God showed his love among us: He sent his one and only Son into the world that we might live through him.

1 JOHN 4:9

*L*ove to one another, says John, is the family likeness of God's children. He who does not love Christians is evidently not in the family, for "God is love" and imparts a loving nature to all who know him (1 John 4:7-8).

But "God is love" is a vague formula. How can we form a clear idea of the love that God would reproduce in us? "He sent his one and only Son into the world . . ." This wasn't done as God's acknowledgment of some real devotion on our part—not at all. "Herein is love, not that we loved God, but that"—in a situation where we did not love him and where there was nothing about us to move him to do anything other than blast and blight us for our ingrained irreligion—"he loved us, and sent his Son to be the propitiation for our sins" (1 John 4:10 KJV). By this divine initiative, says John, the meaning and measure of the love that we must imitate are made known.

Reflect: *What is one way that you can imitate God's love today?*

Monday

Substitution

*Christ redeemed us from the law
by becoming a curse for us.*

GALATIANS 3:13

*P*ropitiation was made by the death of Jesus Christ. "Blood" is a word pointing to the violent death that was inflicted in the animal sacrifices, done by God's own command "to make atonement for yourselves on the altar; it is the blood that makes atonement" (Leviticus 17:11). When Paul tells us that God set forth Jesus to be a propitiation "in his blood" (Romans 3:25), his point is that what quenched God's wrath and so redeemed us from death was not Jesus' life or teaching, not his moral perfection nor his fidelity to the Father as such, but the shedding of his blood in death. Paul explains the atonement in terms of representative substitution—the innocent taking the place of the guilty, in the name and for the sake of the guilty, under the axe of God's judicial retribution. "Christ redeemed us from the law." How? "By becoming a curse for us."

Reflect: *Meditate on the cross—that Jesus substituted for you there, experiencing the Father's wrath in your place.*

Tuesday

Scapegoat

Christ's love compels us, because we are convinced that one died for all.

2 CORINTHIANS 5:14

*R*epresentative substitution, as the way and means of atonement, was taught in typical form by the God-given Old Testament sacrificial system. On the annual Day of Atonement, two goats were used. One was killed as a sin offering in the ordinary way, and the other, after the priest had laid hands on its head and put Israel's sins "on the head" of the animal by confessing them there, was sent away to "bear upon him all their iniquities unto a land not inhabited" (Leviticus 16:21-22 KJV). This double ritual taught a single lesson: that through the sacrifice of a representative substitute God's wrath is averted and sins are borne away out of sight, never to trouble our relationship with God again. The second goat (the scapegoat) illustrates what, in terms of the type, was accomplished by the death of the first goat. These rituals are the immediate background of Paul's teaching on propitiation.

Journal: *Create a drawing, song, poem, or paragraph capturing the blended image of Christ's loving death for our sins and the Old Testament prototype of the two goats.*

Wednesday

The Heart of the Gospel

He was delivered over to death
for our sins and was raised to
life for our justification.

ROMANS 4:25

*T*he gospel tells us that our Creator has become our Redeemer. It announces that the Son of God has become man "for us men and for our salvation" (Nicene Creed, AD 325) and has died on the cross to save us from eternal judgment.

The basic description of the saving death of Christ in the Bible is a *propitiation*. By this means justice is done, because the sins of all who will ever be pardoned were judged and punished in the person of God the Son, and it is on this basis that pardon is now offered to us offenders. Redeeming love and retributive justice joined hands, so to speak, at Calvary, for there God showed himself to be "just, and the justifier of him which believeth in Jesus" (Romans 3:26 KJV).

Do you understand this? If you do, you are now seeing the very heart of the Christian gospel.

Reflect: *What does it mean that God is a just justifier when it comes to your salvation? Respond in a prayer of worship.*

Thursday

On Top of the Truth

Christ loved us and gave himself up for us as a fragrant offering and sacrifice to God.

EPHESIANS 5:2

*W*e have all heard the gospel presented as God's triumphant answer to human problems—problems of our relation with ourselves and our fellow humans and our environment. The gospel does indeed bring us solutions to these problems, but it does so by solving a deeper problem—the deepest of all human problems, the problem of man's relation with his Maker.

Sometimes the death of Christ is depicted as *reconciliation* or *redemption* or a *sacrifice* or an *act of self-giving* or *sin bearing* or *blood shedding*. All of these thoughts have to do with the putting away of sin and the restoring of unclouded fellowship between man and God. They are so many pictures of the reality of propitiation, viewed from different standpoints.

When you stand on top of Mount Snowdon in Wales, you see the whole of Snowdonia spread out around you, and you have a wider view than you can get from any other point in the area. Similarly, when you are on top of the truth of propitiation, you can see the entire Bible in perspective.

Reflect: *Meditate on each of the italicized words above—each reflecting some aspect of God's gift of propitiation to you. Thank him for what they reveal of Christ's love.*

Friday

Among Transgressors

He poured out his life unto death,
and was numbered with the transgressors.

ISAIAH 53:12

*W*hat was the driving force in the life of Jesus? If you sit down for an hour and read straight through the Gospel according to Mark, your basic impression will be that Jesus is a man of action—a man always on the move. Your further impression will be of a man who knew himself to be a divine person (Son of God) fulfilling a messianic role (Son of Man). Going on from this, your impression will be of One whose messianic mission centered on his being put to death—One who was consciously and single-mindedly preparing to die long before the idea of a suffering Messiah took hold of anyone else. Your final impression will be of One for whom this experience of death was a most fearful ordeal.

How should we explain Jesus' belief in the necessity of his death? If we relate the facts in question to the apostolic teaching about propitiation, all becomes plain at once. Jesus was taking on himself the burden of the world's sin, consenting to be, and actually being, numbered among the transgressors.

Reflect: *Spend an hour reading through the book of Mark. Look for what this account of his life reveals of Jesus and his mission.*

Saturday/Sunday

Garden Grief

We considered him striken by God. . . . The punishment that brought us peace was upon him. . . . The LORD has laid on him the iniquity of us all. . . . The LORD makes his life a guilt offering.

ISAIAH 53:4-6, 10

*I*t was because Jesus was made to be sin, and bear God's judgment on sin, that he trembled in the garden. And it was because he was actually bearing that judgment that he declared himself forsaken of God on the cross. Centuries before, Isaiah had spelled it out: "The LORD had laid on him the iniquity of us all." So Anne Cousin (1824–1906) wrote:

> Oh Christ, what burdens bowed Thy head! Our load was
>   laid on Thee;
> Thou stoodest in the sinner's stead, didst bear all ill for me.
> A victim led, Thy blood was shed; now there's no load for me.
>
> The Holy One did hide His face; O Christ, 'twas hid from Thee:
> Dumb darkness wrapped Thy soul a space, the darkness due
>   to me.
> But now that face of radiant grace shines forth in light
>   on me.

Pray: *Respond in prayer to the Isaiah 53 passage, perhaps using the words of the hymn above.*

Monday   *Forsaken*

*My God, my God,
why have you forsaken me?*

Matthew 27:46

$\mathcal{L}$ook at the cross and you see what form God's judicial reaction to human sin will finally take. What form is that? Withdrawal and deprivation of good.

On the cross Jesus lost all the good that he had before. All sense of the Father's presence and love, all sense of physical, mental, and spiritual well-being, all enjoyment of God and of created things, all ease and solace of friendship, were taken from him. In their place was nothing but loneliness, pain, a killing sense of human malice and callousness, and a horror of great spiritual darkness. The physical pain, though great (for crucifixion remains the cruelest form of judicial execution that the world has ever known), was yet only a small part of the story; Jesus' chief sufferings were mental and spiritual. What was packed into less than four hundred minutes was an eternity of agony—agony such that each minute was an eternity in itself, as mental sufferers know that individual minutes can be.

Reflect: *Using a symbol of a cross, meditate on the forsakenness that Jesus endured there. Thank him for that sacrifice.*

Tuesday

God's Peace

In this world you will have trouble.
But take heart! I have overcome the world.

JOHN 16:33

*W*hat does the gospel of God offer us? If we say "the peace of God," none will demur. But will everyone understand?

Too often the peace of God is thought of as if it were essentially a feeling of inner tranquility, happy and carefree, springing from knowledge that God will shield one from life's hardest knocks. But this is a misrepresentation. On the one hand, God does not featherbed his children in this way (and anyone who thinks he does is in for a shock). On the other hand, that which is basic and essential to the real peace of God does not come into this concept at all.

The truth is that God's peace brings us two things: (1) power to face and live with our own badness and failings and (2) contentment under "the slings and arrows of outrageous fortune." The peace *of* God is first and foremost peace *with* God. It is the state of affairs in which God, instead of being *against* us, is *for* us. God's peace is pardon and acceptance into covenant—that is, adoption into God's family.

Journal: *Journal your response to the kind of peace God does (and does not) offer.*

Wednesday

Lamb of God

> *God was pleased . . . through [Christ] to reconcile to himself all things . . . by making peace through his blood, shed on the cross.*

COLOSSIANS 1:19-20

*W*hen Jesus came to his disciples in the upper room at evening on his resurrection day, he said, "Peace be with you." When he had said that, "he showed unto them his hands and side" (John 20:19-20). Why did he do that? Not just to establish his identity, but to remind them of his death on the cross whereby he had made peace with his Father for them.

Having suffered in their place, as their substitute, to make peace for them, he now came in his risen power to bring that peace to them. "Look, the Lamb of God, who takes away the sin of the world!" (John 1:29). It is here in the recognition that, whereas we are by nature at odds with God and God with us, Jesus has made "peace through his blood, shed on the cross" (Colossians 1:20) that true knowledge of God begins.

Reflect: *If you had been in that upper room on resurrection night, what new meaning would God's peace take on for you?*

Thursday

Knowing Love

I pray that you, being rooted and established in love, may have power, together with all the saints, to grasp how wide and long and high and deep is the love of Christ, and to know this love that surpasses knowledge.

EPHESIANS 3:17-19

*P*aul prays that the readers of his Ephesian letter may "know [God's] love that surpasses knowledge" (Ephesians 3:18-19). The touch of incoherence and paradox in his language reflects Paul's sense that the reality of divine love is inexpressibly great. Nevertheless, he believes that some comprehension of it can be reached. How? The answer of Ephesians is a review of the whole plan of grace set forth in the first two chapters of the letter (election, redemption, regeneration, preservation, and glorification), of which the atoning sacrifice of Christ is the centerpiece.

Christ's sacrifice of himself on our behalf is the demonstration and measure of his love for us, the love that we are to imitate in our dealings with each other. "Live a life of love, just as Christ loved us and gave himself up for us as a fragrant offering and sacrifice to God" (Ephesians 5:2).

Pray: *Pray Paul's prayer above, attaching the name of someone you want to receive this blessing from God.*

Friday

The Qualities of Love

*Christ loved the church and gave himself up
for her to make her holy, cleansing her by the
washing with water through the word, and to
present her to himself as a radiant church,
without stain or wrinkle or any other blemish,
but holy and blameless.*

EPHESIANS 5:25-27

*C*hrist's love was *free,* not elicited by any goodness in us
(Ephesians 2:1-5). It was *eternal,* being one with the choice to
save sinners that the Father made "before the creation of the
world" (Ephesians 1:4). It was *unreserved,* for it led him down to
the depths of humiliation and, indeed, of hell itself on Calvary.
And it was *sovereign,* for it has achieved its object—the final glory
of the redeemed, for their perfect holiness and happiness in the
fruition of his love (Ephesians 5:26-27) is now guaranteed and
assured (Ephesians 4:30). Dwell on these things, Paul urges, if
you would catch a sight, however dim, of the greatness and the
glory of divine love.

Journal: *Ephesians shows God's love as* free, eternal, unreserved,
and sovereign. *Write how each of these characteristics of God's love
influences your own spiritual condition here and now.*

Saturday/Sunday   *Calvary's Glory*

*Now is the Son of Man glorified
and God is glorified in him.*

JOHN 13:31

*I*n the upper room, after Judas had gone out into the night to betray him, Jesus said, "Now is the Son of Man glorified." What did he mean?

"Son of Man" was Jesus' name for himself as the Savior-King who, before being enthroned, must fulfill Isaiah 53. When he spoke of the present glorifying of the Son of Man, and of God in him, he was thinking specifically of the atoning death, the "lifting up" on the cross, which Judas had gone to precipitate.

Do you see the glory of God, in his wisdom, power, righteousness, truth, and love, supremely disclosed at Calvary in the making of propitiation for our sins? The Bible does. We venture to add that, if you felt the burden and pressure of your own sins in their true weight, so would you.

Reflect: *Meditatively, read Isaiah 53, looking for the mysterious glory of the cross. Pray your thanks for God's propitiation as it is revealed there.*

Monday

Heaven's Praise

Worthy is the Lamb, who was slain, to receive power and wealth and wisdom and strength and honor and glory and praise!

REVELATION 5:12

*I*n heaven, where Christ's redeeming work is better understood than here, angels and people unite to praise "the Lamb who was slain." Here on earth, those who by grace have been made spiritual realists do the same.

Bearing shame and scoffing rude in my place condemned
     He stood;
Sealed my pardon with His blood: Hallelujah! What a Savior!
("Man of Sorrows")

He left his Father's throne above, so free, so infinite His grace;
Emptied Himself of all but love and bled for Adam's
     helpless race.
Amazing love! How can it be? For O, my God, it found out me!
("And Can It Be")

Pray: *Using one or both of the songs above, consciously join heavenly beings in their ongoing praise of God.*

Tuesday

Knowing Glory

God, who said, "Let light shine out of darkness," made his light shine in our hearts to give us the light of the knowledge of the glory of God in the face of Christ.

2 CORINTHIANS 4:6

If Thou has my discharge procured, and freely in my
    room endured
  The whole of wrath divine,
Payment God cannot twice demand, first at my bleeding
    Surety's hand,
  and then again at mine.
Turn then, my soul, unto thy rest; the merits of thy great
    High Priest
  have bought thy liberty.
Trust in His efficacious blood, Nor fear thy banishment
    from God,
  Since Jesus died for Thee!

This is the song of the heirs of heaven, those who have seen "the light of the knowledge of the glory of God in the face [that is, the person, office, and achievement] of Christ." The joyful news of redeeming love and saving mercy, which is the heart of the gospel, spurs them to never-ending praise. Let us join their worship.

Reflect: *What insights do you find in the hymn above that can aid your own worship?*

Wednesday

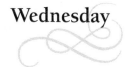

God's Wisdom

[God's] wisdom is profound,
his power is vast.

JOB 9:4

*W*hat does the Bible mean when it calls God wise? In Scripture, wisdom is a moral as well as an intellectual quality, more than mere intelligence or knowledge, just as it is more than mere cleverness or cunning. For us to be truly wise, in the Bible sense, our intelligence and cleverness must be harnessed to a right end.

Wisdom is the power to see, and the inclination to choose, the best and highest goal, together with the surest means of attaining it. Wisdom is, in fact, the practical side of moral goodness. As such, it is found in its fullness only in God. He alone is naturally and entirely and invariably wise. "His wisdom ever waketh," says the old hymn, and it is true.

God is never other than wise in anything that he does. Wisdom, as the old theologians used to say, is his essence. Just as power and truth and goodness are his essence—integral elements, that is, in his character.

Reflect: *Consider wisdom as it is described here. How have you seen this to be true of God? In what ways would you like to see this wisdom become part of your own character?*

Thursday

Wisdom and Power

To God belong wisdom and power.

JOB 12:13

*H*uman wisdom can be frustrated by circumstantial factors outside the wise person's control. Power is as much God's essence as wisdom is. Omniscience governing omnipotence, infinite power ruled by infinite wisdom is a basic biblical description of the divine character. "His *wisdom* is profound, his *power* is vast" (Job 9:4). "To God belong *wisdom* and *power*" (Job 12:13). "He is mighty in *strength* and *wisdom*" (Job 36:5 KJV). He has "great *power* and mighty *strength* . . . and his *understanding* no one can fathom" (Isaiah 40:26, 28). "*Wisdom and power* are his" (Daniel 2:20). The same conjunction appears in the New Testament: "Now to him that is of *power* to stablish you according to my gospel . . . God only *wise*" (Romans 16:25, 27 KJV).

Wisdom without power would be pathetic, a broken reed. Power without wisdom would be merely frightening. But in God boundless wisdom and endless power are united, and this makes him utterly worthy of our fullest trust.

Reflect: *How does God's wisdom and his power (coupled together) help you to trust him? What current uncertainty can you handle more faithfully because of this trust?*

Friday

A Life of Ease

Though he slay me,
yet will I hope in him.

JOB 13:15

*G*od's almighty wisdom is always active and never fails. All his works of creation and providence and grace display it, and until we can see it in them, we just are not seeing them straight. But we cannot recognize God's wisdom unless we know the end for which he is working.

Here many go wrong. Misunderstanding what the Bible means when it says that God is love (see 1 John 4:8-10), they think that God intends a trouble-free life for all. Hence they conclude that anything painful and upsetting (illness, accident, injury, job loss, the suffering of a loved one) indicates either that God's wisdom or his power, or both, have broken down. Or they conclude that God, after all, does not exist.

But this idea of God's intention is a complete mistake. God's wisdom is not pledged to keep a fallen world happy. Not even to Christians has he promised a trouble-free life; rather the reverse. He has other ends in view for life in this world than simply to make it easy for everyone.

Journal: *What are some of your reactions to trouble? What do you hope your responses to trouble might become?*

Saturday/Sunday

God's Glory

> *Love the LORD your God with all your heart and with all your soul and with all your strength.*

DEUTERONOMY 6:5

*W*hen God made us, his purpose was that we should love and honor him, praising him for the wonderfully ordered complexity and variety of his world, using it according to his will, and so enjoying both it and him. And though we have fallen, God has not abandoned his first purpose. Still he plans that a great host of humankind should come to love and honor him. His ultimate objective is to bring them to a state in which they please him entirely and praise him adequately, a state in which he is all in all to them, and he and they rejoice continually in the knowledge of each other's love—people rejoicing in the saving love of God, set upon them from all eternity, and God rejoicing in the responsive love of people, drawn out of them by grace through the gospel. This is God's *glory*, our *glory* too, in every sense that that weighty word can bear.

Reflect: *Consider your love of God. Even in your quiet moments of fear, loneliness, or worry, how can your love of God become his "glory"?*

Monday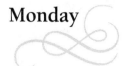

Glory Here

> *I have given them the glory*
> *that you gave me, that they*
> *may be one as we are one.*

JOHN 17:22

*G*od's glory will be fully realized only in the next world, in the context of a transformation of the whole created order. Meanwhile, however, God works steadily toward it. His immediate objectives are to draw individual men and women into a relationship of faith, hope, and love toward himself, delivering them from sin and showing forth in their lives the power of his grace; to defend his people against the forces of evil; and to spread throughout the world the gospel by means of which he saves. In the fulfillment of each part of this purpose the Lord Jesus Christ is central, for God has set him forth both as Savior from sin, whom we must trust, and as Lord of the church, whom we must obey. It is in the light of this complex purpose that the wisdom of God in his dealings with individuals is to be seen.

Journal: *The text above admits that God's purposes are "complex." Thoughtfully reread the paragraph, noting as many purposes as you can find. Journal, to the best of your ability, your current place in these purposes.*

Tuesday

Abraham

*Whom have I in heaven but you? And
earth has nothing I desire besides you. . . .
God is the strength of my heart.*

PSALM 73:25-26

Abraham was not by nature a man of strong principle, and his sense of responsibility was somewhat deficient. His repeated shabby deceptions actually endangered his wife's chastity (Genesis 12:10-20). Lacking moral courage, he was altogether too anxious about his own personal security (Genesis 12:12-13; 20:11).

Again and again God confronted Abraham with himself and so led Abraham to the point where his heart could say, with the psalmist, "Whom have I in heaven but you?" And as the story proceeds, we see in Abraham's life the results of his learning this lesson. The old weaknesses still sometimes reappear, but alongside them emerges a new nobility and independence, the outworking of Abraham's developed habit of walking with God, resting in his revealed will, relying on him, waiting for him, bowing to his providence, obeying him even when he commands something odd and unconventional. From being a man of the world, Abraham becomes a man of God.

Pray: *What do you see of yourself in Abraham? Talk to God about it. If you are honestly able, pray the words of Psalm 73:25-26.*

Wednesday

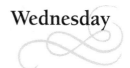

Jacob

In the course of my life
[God] broke my strength.

PSALM 102:23

*J*acob, Abraham's grandson, was a self-willed mother's boy, blessed (or cursed) with all the opportunist instincts and amoral ruthlessness of a go-getting businessman. But God in his wisdom resolved to instill true religion into Jacob. Jacob must be weaned away from trust in his own cleverness to dependence on God, and he must be made to abhor the unscrupulous double-dealing that came so naturally to him. Jacob, therefore, must be made to feel his own utter weakness, must be brought to such complete self-distrust that he would no longer try to get on by exploiting others.

With patient wisdom (for God always waits for the right time), God led Jacob to the point at which he could stamp the required sense of impotent helplessness indelibly and decisively on Jacob's soul. After decades of patient teaching, God wrestled with Jacob and *lamed* him (Genesis 32:25), putting his thigh out of joint to be a perpetual reminder in his flesh of his own spiritual weakness and his need to lean always on God, just as for the rest of his life he had to walk leaning on a stick.

Reflect: *How do your own weaknesses draw you to lean on God?*

Thursday   *Joseph*

The word of the LORD tried him.

PSALM 105:19 KJV

*Y*oung Joseph's brothers sold him to slavery in Egypt, where, traduced by Potiphar's venomous wife, he was wrongly imprisoned, though afterward he rose to eminence. For what purpose? So far as Joseph personally was concerned, the answer is given in Psalm 105:19: "the word of the LORD *tried* him." Joseph was being tested, refined, and matured. He was being taught during his spell as a slave, and in prison, to stay himself in God, to remain cheerful and charitable in frustrating circumstances, and to wait patiently for the Lord. So far as the life of God's people was concerned, Joseph himself gave the answer to our question when he revealed his identity to his distracted brothers. "But God sent me ahead of you to preserve for you a remnant on earth and to save your lives by a great deliverance. So then, it was not you who sent me here, but God" (Genesis 45:7-8).

Once again we are confronted with the wisdom of God ordering the events of a human life for a double purpose: the individual's own personal sanctification and the fulfilling of his appointed ministry and service in the life of the people of God.

Reflect: *How do you see God's two purposes (identified above) in events of your own life?*

Friday

Tested Gold

*[God] knows the way that
I take; when he has tested me,
I will come forth as gold.*

JOB 23:10

The same wisdom that ordered the paths that God's saints trod in Bible times orders the Christian's life today. We should not, therefore, be too taken aback when unexpected and upsetting and discouraging things happen to us now. What do they mean? Simply that God in his wisdom means to make something of us that we have not yet attained. Perhaps he means to strengthen us in patience, good humor, compassion, humility, or meekness by giving us practice in exercising these graces under especially difficult conditions. Perhaps he has a new lesson in self-denial and self-distrust to teach us. Perhaps he wishes to break us of complacency, unreality, or undetected forms of pride and conceit. Perhaps his purpose is simply to draw us closer to himself, for it is often the case that fellowship with the Father and the Son is most vivid, and Christian joy is greatest, when the cross is heaviest. Or perhaps God is preparing us for forms of service of which at present we have no inkling.

Pray: *What personal hope, and what apprehension, do you find in the paragraph above? Bring these to God in prayer.*

Saturday/Sunday   *Holding On to Trust*

*[God] comforts us in all our
troubles, so that we can comfort those
in any trouble with the comfort we
ourselves have received from God.*

2 CORINTHIANS 1:4

*E*ven Jesus "learned . . . obedience by the things which he suffered" and so was "made perfect" for his high priestly ministry
(Hebrews 5:8-9 KJV). This means that he is able to uphold us
and make us more than conquerors in all our troubles. We must
not be surprised if Jesus calls us to follow in his steps and to let
ourselves be prepared for the service of others by painful experiences that are quite undeserved. We may be frankly bewildered
at things that happen to us, but God knows exactly what he is
doing, and what he is after, in his handling of our affairs. Always
and in everything he is wise—we shall see that hereafter, even
where we never saw it here. (Job in heaven knows the full reason
why he was afflicted, though he never knew it in this life.) Meanwhile, we ought not to hesitate to trust God's wisdom, even when
he leaves us in the dark.

Reflect: *What painful events do you need to trust to God's
wisdom? How can you comfort others because of them?*

Monday 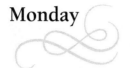 *Sufficient Grace*

*My grace is sufficient for you, for
my power is made perfect in weakness.*

2 CORINTHIANS 12:9

*H*ow are we to meet baffling and trying situations if we cannot for the moment see God's purpose in them? First, by taking them as from God and asking ourselves what reactions to them—and in them—the gospel of God requires of us. Second, by seeking God's face specifically about them.

If we do those two things, we will never find ourselves wholly in the dark as to God's purpose in our troubles. We will always be able to see at least as much purpose in them as Paul was enabled to see in his thorn in the flesh (whatever it was). It came to him, he tells us, as a "messenger of Satan" (2 Corinthians 12:7), tempting him to hard thoughts of God. He resisted this temptation and sought Christ's face three times, asking that it might be removed. The only answer he had was this: "My grace is sufficient for you, for my power is made perfect in weakness" (verse 9).

Journal: *What do you think of these two responses to trying situations? Do you find them natural or difficult? Resolve to make these two responses in a current difficult situation. Journal the results.*

Tuesday

Humble Boasting

I will boast all the more gladly about my weaknesses, so that Christ's power may rest on me.

2 CORINTHIANS 12:9

*P*aul's attitude in the Scripture above is a model for us. On reflection, he perceived a reason why he should have been afflicted with a "thorn." It was "to keep me from becoming conceited because of these surpassingly great revelations" (2 Corinthians 12:7). Whatever further purpose a Christian's troubles may or may not have in equipping him for future service, they will always have at least the purpose that Paul's thorn in the flesh had: they will have been sent to make and keep us humble and to give us a new opportunity of showing forth the power of Christ in our mortal lives. Is not this enough in itself to convince us of the wisdom of God in them?

Once Paul saw that his trouble was sent to enable him to glorify Christ, he accepted it as wisely appointed and even rejoiced in it. God give us grace, in all our own troubles, to go and do likewise.

Reflect: *Are you able to allow trouble to produce godly humility in you, or do you fight it, hoping to keep your pride intact?*

Wednesday

Hope and Life

> *May the God of hope fill you with all*
> *joy and peace as you trust in him,*
> *so that you may overflow with hope*
> *by the power of the Holy Spirit.*

ROMANS 15:13

I have been a believer for more than half a century, but only recently have I appreciated how pastorally profound Paul's prayer was—and is. While there is life, there's hope, we say, but the deeper truth is that only while there's hope is there life. Take away hope, and life, with all its fascinating variety of opportunities and experiences, reduces to mere existence—uninteresting, ungratifying, bleak, drab, and repellent, a burden and a pain.

People without hope often express their sense of reality and their feelings about themselves by saying they wish they were dead, and sometimes they make attempts on their own life. Hope generates energy, enthusiasm, and excitement; lack of hope breeds only apathy and inertia. So for fully developed (as distinct from partly diminished) humanness, there needs to be hope in our hearts.

Reflect: *What connections have you noticed between hope and your feelings about life? What difference would it make if you could at this moment "overflow with hope"?*

Thursday

Hope Through Uncertainty

*Faith is being sure of what
we hope for and certain
of what we do not see.*

HEBREWS 11:1

*T*rue hope is rooted in God.

Years ago the wife of a man I knew as a student published a testimony about the day her husband lost his job: "I shall never forget Francis's face as he walked through our front door that evening. . . . It was quite gray and utterly defeated. . . . He was willing to do any work at all . . . but no one wanted him. It hurt me to see a man usually so full of vigor aimlessly staring into space."

Later with a group of friends: "While we had been praying he had felt a change come over him. Hope had sprung up within him and with it decisions, ideas, action. . . . I do not know why Francis lost his job. I do not know why he is doing well now. But I do know that I can trust God. . . . And after faith and love, hope is one of his most precious gifts to mankind."

Pray: *What do you currently find most unsettling? Ask God for his gift of hope.*

Friday

Hope in the Dark

Be of good courage, and [God]
shall strengthen your heart.

PSALM 31:24 KJV

*E*ven when hopelessness is only fitful and intermittent, a mood that possesses until it passes, it still makes us feel alone, afraid, and paralyzed for action. We find that we cannot make decisions nor bring ourselves to do things. Our sense of self-worth dissolves into self-doubt, self-distrust, and self-dislike. Confidence is swallowed up by despair. We are in a tunnel that has no light at the end of it, only deeper darkness and eventually a blank wall.

We human beings are so made that we live in our own fancied future. This is not a policy decision but simply the way we are. To look forward, to dream of happy things to come, to want what is good to continue and what is bad to end, and to long for a future that is better than the past, is as natural as breathing.

Journal: *Are you (or a friend) in the dark tunnel described above? What places you there? What are some spiritually wise coping mechanisms? How can hope in the Lord become a light at the end of that tunnel?*

Saturday/Sunday   *Hope in Hopeless Times*

Christic in you, the hope of glory.

COLOSSIANS 1:27

The philosopher Immanuel Kant said that one of life's three basic questions is, what may we hope for? He was right.

The twentieth century opened in optimism. The ruling assumption was that we are all basically good and wise, and advancing Christian civilization would soon make the kingdom of God (understood as universal neighborly love) a global reality. A periodical called *The Christian Century* was founded to channel these hopes and chronicle their fulfillment. It still exists, but its title now seems woefully inept.

As the third millennium opened, many thoughtful people entered the twenty-first century with fear rather than hope, wondering how far the educated, affluent, and technologically equipped decadence of the West would go and what sort of a world awaits our grandchildren.

What follows? Is there nothing good to hope for at all? There is, but we must seek this good hope outside the socio-politico-economic process. God the Creator, who designed us, sustains us and knows our hearts, never intended that humans should live without hope.

Reflect: *Carefully read Colossians 1:24-29. What do you find here that inspires you to live in hope even in a post-Christian environment?*

Monday

A Book of Hope

He who testifies to these things
says, "Yes, I am coming soon."
Amen. Come, Lord Jesus.

REVELATION 22:20

*A*s God the Father is a God of hope, so his incarnate Son, Jesus of Nazareth, crucified, risen, reigning, and returning, is a messenger, means, and mediator of hope. The Bible—"God's Word written," as the Anglican doctrinal standard, the Thirty-Nine Articles, describes it—is from Genesis to Revelation a book of hope. The first recorded divine promise, that the woman's seed would crush the serpent's head, was a word of hope in the Garden of Eden (Genesis 3:15). The last recorded promise of Jesus, "I am coming soon" (Revelation 22:20), was a word of hope for churches facing persecution. Hope, the guaranteed expectation enabling believers to look forward with joy, is in truth one of the great themes of Christianity and one of the supreme gifts of God.

Pray: *Page through any random section of the Bible, pausing to read now and then and looking for signs of hope. Thank God for what you find there.*

Tuesday

A Place of Hope

Christ [loves] the church—for
we are members of his body.

EPHESIANS 5:29-30

What the Bible tells us about hope, in a nutshell, is this: humans were originally created in fellowship with God so that we might exalt and enjoy him forever, first for a probationary period in this world and then in a place of "eternal pleasures" (Psalm 16:11) that is off the map of this space-time universe. When sin infected our race, disrupting this fellowship, robbing us all of the hope of heaven and bringing us under the threat of hell, our Creator acted to form a forgiven and reborn human race. This is the church, a community that should enjoy humankind's original destiny—and more—through sovereign divine grace and personal faith in our Lord Jesus Christ.

Journal: *What are some ways that you find hope within your church? What are some ways that you can become an instrument of hope within your church? (Consider hope for the here and now as well as hope for eternity.)*

Wednesday

Hopeful Waiting

By faith we eagerly await through the Spirit the righteousness for which we hope.

GALATIANS 5:5

*B*elievers in every age should live in the knowledge that they are God's adopted children and heirs of what is spoken of as his glory, his city, and his kingdom. They should know that Jesus Christ, who out of love gave his life for the church inclusively (Ephesians 5:25) and for each future believer personally (Galatians 2:20), is now with them individually by his Spirit (Matthew 28:20) to care for them daily as a shepherd for his sheep (John 10:2-4) and to strengthen them constantly according to their need (Philippians 4:13). He will finally take them from this world to see and share the heavenly bliss that is already his (John 14:1-3). With Paul, therefore, they should "eagerly await through the Spirit the righteousness for which we hope" (Galatians 5:5). The Christian identity is not only that of a believer but that of a hoper too.

Reflect: *What current circumstances diminish your hope? What do you find in the paragraph above that helps you (even in those circumstances) to wait with hope?*

Thursday

Two Hopes

As in Adam all die, so in
Christ all will be made alive.

1 CORINTHIANS 15:22

*T*he word *hope* signifies two distinct, though related, realities. Objectively it means the divinely guaranteed prospect before us. Subjectively it means the activity or habit of looking forward to the day when what is promised will become ours in actual enjoyment. It is thus quite distinct from optimism.

Optimism hopes for the best without any guarantee of its arriving and is often no more than whistling in the dark. Christian hope, by contrast, is faith looking ahead to the fulfillment of the promises of God, as when the Anglican burial service inters the corpse "in sure and certain hope of the Resurrection to eternal life, through our Lord Jesus Christ." Christian hope expresses knowledge that each day of his life, and every moment beyond it, the believer can say with truth, on the basis of God's own commitment, that the best is yet to come.

Journal: *How does the prospect that you will die in hope help you to live with hope?*

Friday

Joyful Hoping

*We rejoice in the hope
of the glory of God.*

ROMANS 5:2

*C*hristian hoping, by virtue of its object (the guaranteed, never-ending generosity of God), calls forth love, joy, zeal, initiative, and devoted action. Therefore, as C. S. Lewis put it, those who have done the most for the present world have been those who thought most of the next.

Paul himself, in Romans, displays the reality of this. He presents Abraham as a model of justifying faith because he believed a promise of God shaping his future that at the time seemed too good to be truth. "Against all hope, Abraham in hope believed, . . . being fully persuaded that God had power to do what he had promised" (Romans 4:18, 21). Describing the life of those justified by faith, he writes, "We rejoice in the hope of the glory of God" (5:2) and "Be joyful in hope" (12:12).

Journal: *What makes you joyful? In five minutes, jot a quick "joy list." Circle one item on that list and write a paragraph about it, drawing connections between joy and hope.*

Saturday/Sunday

Hope Notes

*Everything that was written in
the past was written to teach us, so that
through endurance and the encouragement
of the Scriptures we might have hope.*

ROMANS 15:4

We learn from Paul that as we have been saved in one sense, so we shall be saved in another. Salvation is both now and not yet. We should thank God for it in the former sense, in which it becomes ours upon our believing (Romans 1:16; 6:17-18, 22-23; 11:11, 14), while we await its coming in the latter sense, confident that every day brings it nearer (13:11). Then in 15:4 Paul tells us strikingly that "everything that was written in the past [that is, all of what we call the Old Testament] was written to teach us [he means us Christian believers], so that through endurance and the encouragement of the Scriptures we might have hope." And in 15:13, he prays that the "God of hope" will enable his readers to "overflow with hope" as they take these things to heart.

Journal: *Study each passage above, looking for what builds hope within you. In your journal, write "hope notes" to yourself based on each passage.*

Monday 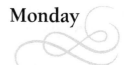 *Servants of Hope*

We are . . . Christ's ambassadors,
as though God were making
his appeal through us.

2 CORINTHIANS 5:20

A truth of which healthy, growing Christians become more and more aware is that God is transcendently great and the human individual by comparison is infinitely insignificant. God, we realize, can get on very well without any of us. So it should give us an overwhelming sense of privilege that not only has he made, loved, and saved us but also he takes us as his working partners for advancing his plans. Thus Paul can call his colleagues and himself "Christ's ambassadors" and God's "fellow workers" (2 Corinthians 5:20; 6:1), and he tells us to see ourselves in our own sphere as servants, ministers, and workers of God.

And none of us is excluded, for Scripture shows God using the oddest, rawest, most lopsided and flawed of his children to further his work. This is a fact of enormous encouragement to sensitive souls who feel they are not fit to serve him.

Reflect: *Slowly read the words of 2 Corinthians 5:20. As you think of people you will encounter during the coming day, how can you live this one day "as though God were making his appeal" through you?*

Tuesday   *Battle for Hope*

Praise be to the God and Father of our Lord Jesus Christ! In his great mercy he has given us new birth into a living hope through the resurrection of Jesus Christ from the dead.

1 PETER 1:3

*H*ope is a tender plant, easily crushed and extinguished. Every believer can count on having moments of disappointment and frustration, when we say and feel that things are hopeless.

The speeches of traumatized Job as he sat among the ashes, sick, bewildered, and hurting in his mind as well as his body, express the death of hope in classic terms. "Who can see any hope for me?" (Job 17:15). Job, though finally restored in material terms (42:10), could receive no basis for hope from God other than the message "Trust me to know what I'm doing."

But Christians know more than Job knew, and Peter sets before us resources for the reviving of hope in our hearts whenever it is threatened. "Praise be to the God and Father of our Lord Jesus Christ! In his great mercy he has given us new birth into a living hope."

Reflect: *When do you have to battle to maintain hope? How can you go about that battle?*

Wednesday

Practicing Hope

*May our Lord Jesus Christ himself and God
our Father, who loved us and by his grace
gave us eternal encouragement and good
hope, encourage your hearts and strengthen
you in every good deed and word.*

2 THESSALONIANS 2:16-17

$\mathcal{T}$o stifle hope as a habit of mind and heart, Satan exploits both
our inbuilt weaknesses of character and our acquired defects of
attitude and behavior that testify to bad and failed relationships
in our past. Thus some of us have a temperament that is naturally
gloomy so that we are filled with self-absorption and self-pity.
Feeling beached and abandoned and expecting the worst come
naturally to us—as they did to Eeyore in the saga of Winnie-the-
Pooh. Emotional exhaustion over any length of time leaves us
feeling, as a man once said to me, that our faith is as fragile as
tissue paper. Hoping for anything is simply beyond us. Satan is
a master at using these and similar conditions to keep us from
the practice of hope. But the heart of the Christian hope, both
here and hereafter, is the saved sinner's loving fellowship with
the Father, the Son, and the Holy Spirit.

Journal: *In writing, instruct yourself in "the practice of hope."
Page back through the past dozen devotionals looking for ideas.
Then write.*

Thursday

Hope from Samson

> *I do not have time to tell about
> Gideon, Barak, Samson, . . . whose
> weakness was turned to strength.*

HEBREWS 11:32, 34

*N*o one, surely, can read the Samson story without thinking, *This is tragedy.* Tragedy is a waste of good, a squandering of potential—and this is a picture of Samson. The story of Samson's life is much like the sort of thing you read in paperback thrillers: women and fights all the way. But there's a message here for us. We must seek to get our lives—and keep our lives—in a shape that will glorify God. It means fighting our sins, disciplining our thoughts, changing our attitudes, and criticizing our desires in a way that Samson did not try to do. But God used him anyway! Let's trust in the Lord who uses flawed human material for his glory. Those who seek, find, for Samson's God, who is our God, is a God of great patience and great grace. Thus there is great hope for us all.

Pray: *In prayer, bring to God your own weaknesses. Invite him to strengthen what he wills to strengthen and then to use even your flaws for his glory.*

Friday

Hope from Jacob

> *[Joseph said to his brothers,]*
> *"You intended to harm me, but God*
> *intended it for good to accomplish*
> *what is now being done, the*
> *saving of many lives."*

GENESIS 50:20

*J*acob was a grabber, an exploiter, a manipulator, and a cheat. He was an uninhibited, self-centered go-getter who made enemies even (perhaps especially) among his own family. But because Jacob had a heart for God as well as for gain, God mercifully guided him, guarded him, and changed him for the better.

We serve a God who loves us, and we're to interpret everything that happens to us in terms of the love of God. But if we feel that we have failed our God and our own families, we must remember that as Christians we live by being forgiven. Our God is endlessly gracious. As there was recovery first for Jacob and then for his family, including Joseph, so there is hope in God for us and ours.

Pray: *Focus prayer on one member of your family who has been hurt by your flaws. Ask for God's forgiveness for you, for his care for that person, and for hope for both of you.*

Saturday/Sunday *Hope from Jonah*

You are a gracious and compassionate God,
slow to anger and abounding in love,
a God who relents from sending calamity.

JONAH 4:2

*G*od taught Jonah two key lessons: the lesson of obedience and the lesson of compassion. It was discipline for Jonah to be swallowed by the fish. It was discipline for Jonah to have his precious vine wither and fall at his feet.

Let us learn to be glad that our God, Jonah's God, is "a gracious and compassionate God." As God set himself to change Jonah into a man of compassion, so let us allow him to teach us to be men and women of compassion—neighbor lovers in the fullest sense. Arrogance and anger must somehow be squeezed out of us before we can truly hope in God—by practicing obedience as the good way for us and leaving global politics and history in his wise, generous, and merciful hands—and God does this for us. In the book of Jonah we see him doing it for Jonah, and in that narrative lies the assurance that he will do it for us too.

Reflect: *In what settings do you most need to learn obedience toward God and compassion toward people? Ask God to make you a willing student of Jonah's lessons.*

Monday   *Hope from Thomas*

Thomas said to him, "My Lord and my God!"
Then Jesus told him, "Because you have seen
me, you have believed; blessed are those who
have not seen and yet have believed."

JOHN 20:28-29

Thomas said, "Unless I see the nail marks in his hands and put my finger where the nails were, . . . I will not believe it" (John 20:25). This was the evening of the day that changed the world quite literally—the day when Jesus died as a sacrifice for our sins, rose from the dead, and showed himself alive and well again on planet Earth.

Jesus was gentle with Thomas. He said in effect, "If it is going to help you to touch the wounds in my body, then do it."

Thomas was absolutely broken. "My Lord, and my God!" he said. And in saying that, he made the perfect confession of faith.

John ends this chapter by saying, "These [signs] are written that you may believe that Jesus is the Christ, the Son of God, and that by believing you may have life in his name" (John 20:31).

Pray: *Jesus patiently guided Thomas from doubt to faith—and with that faith brought hope. Thank God for his patience with you. Ask for the gift of hope.*

Tuesday

Transcendent God

"My thoughts are not your thoughts,
neither are your ways my ways,"
declares the LORD.

ISAIAH 55:8

When the old Reformed theologians dealt with the attributes of God, they used to classify them in two groups: *incommunicable* and *communicable*. In the first group, they put those qualities that highlight God's transcendence and show how vastly different a being he is from us, his creatures. The usual list included God's *independence* (self-existence and self-sufficiency); his *immutability* (entire freedom from change, leading to entire consistency in action); his *infinity* (freedom from all limits of time and space, that is, his eternity and omnipresence); and his *simplicity* (the fact that there are in him no elements that can conflict so that, unlike us, he cannot be torn in different directions by divergent thoughts and desires). The theologians called these qualities *incommunicable* because they are characteristic of God alone. Humans, just because they are human and not God, do not and cannot share any of them.

Journal: *Carefully reread the paragraph above. Write any questions that come to mind.*

Wednesday

Image of God

God created man in his own image,
in the image of God he created him;
male and female he created them.

GENESIS 1:27

*N*ot all of God's qualities belong to him alone. He shares some of his attributes with humans.

Early theologians lumped together qualities like God's spirituality, freedom, and omnipotence, along with his moral attributes—goodness, truth, holiness, righteousness, and so on. What was the principle of classification here? It was this: when God made man, he *communicated* to him qualities corresponding to all of these. This is what the Bible means when it tells us that God made man in his own image, namely that God made man a free spiritual being, a responsible moral agent with powers of choice and action, able to communicate with him and respond to him, and by nature good, truthful, holy, and upright (Ecclesiastes 7:29). In a word, godly.

Journal: *When have you seen the image of God reflected in another person? What have you been thankful for in that image?*

Thursday

Restored Image

We, who with unveiled faces all reflect the Lord's glory, are being transformed into his likeness with ever-increasing glory, which comes from the Lord, who is the Spirit.

2 CORINTHIANS 3:18

*T*he moral qualities that belonged to the divine image were lost at the Fall. God's image in man has been universally defaced, for all humankind has in one way or another lapsed into ungodliness. But the Bible tells us that now, in fulfillment of his plan of redemption, God is at work in Christian believers to repair his ruined image by communicating these qualities to them afresh. This is what Scripture means when it says Christians are being renewed in the image of Christ (2 Corinthians 3:18) and of God (Colossians 3:10).

Among these communicable attributes, the theologians put wisdom. As God is wise in himself, so he imparts wisdom to his creatures.

Journal: *Whose wisdom has helped guide you toward being renewed in the image of Christ? Describe times when you have seen the image of Christ in this person, then write your thankfulness.*

Friday    *Finding Wisdom*

*If any of you lacks wisdom, he should
ask God, . . . and it will be given to him.*

JAMES 1:5

*T*he Bible has a great deal to say about the divine gift of wisdom.

The first nine chapters of the book of Proverbs are a single sustained exhortation to seek this gift. "Wisdom is supreme; therefore get wisdom. Though it cost all you have, get understanding" (Proverbs 4:7). The emphasis throughout is on God's readiness to give wisdom (pictured as wisdom's readiness to give herself) to all who desire the gift and will take the steps necessary to obtain it.

Similar emphases appear in the New Testament. Wisdom is required of Christians: "Live—not as unwise but as wise. . . . Do not be foolish, but understand what the Lord's will is" (Ephesians 5:15-17). "Be wise in the way you act toward outsiders" (Colossians 4:5). And James, in God's name, makes a promise: "If any of you lacks wisdom, he should ask God, . . . and it will be given to him" (James 1:5).

Pray: *Ask God to give you wisdom—and also to help you recognize wisdom when he gives it.*

Saturday/Sunday

Fearing God

*The fear of the LORD is
the beginning of wisdom.*

PROVERBS 9:10

*R*everential fear of God is a good start on wisdom. Not till we have become humble and teachable, standing in awe of God's holiness and sovereignty ("the great and awesome God," Nehemiah 1:5), acknowledging our own littleness, distrusting our own thoughts, and willing to have our minds turned upside down, can divine wisdom become ours. It is to be feared that many Christians spend all their lives in too un-humbled and conceited a frame of mind ever to gain wisdom from God. Not for nothing does Scripture say, "With the lowly is wisdom" (Proverbs 11:2 KJV).

Journal: *Make a list of some of your current worries and fears. How might your awe of God lead you toward a wise way of coping with those fears? Ask God for that kind of wisdom.*

Monday
Dwelling Richly

Let the word of Christ dwell in you richly.

COLOSSIANS 3:16

*W*isdom is divinely wrought in those, and those only, who apply themselves to God's revelation. So Paul admonishes the Colossians, "Let the *word of Christ* dwell in you richly . . . with all wisdom" (Colossians 3:16).

How are we of the twenty-first century to do this? By soaking ourselves in the Scriptures. Yet it is to be feared that many today who profess to be Christ's never learn wisdom due to their failure to attend sufficiently to God's written Word.

Cranmer's Prayer Book lectionary (which all Anglicans are meant to follow) will take one through the Old Testament once and the New Testament twice every year. William Gouge, the Puritan, read fifteen chapters regularly each day. How long has it been since you read right through the Bible? Do you spend as much time with the Bible each day as you do with the news?

What fools some of us are! And we remain fools all our lives, simply because we will not take the trouble to do what has to be done to receive the wisdom that is God's free gift.

Reflect: *Ask yourself each question above. Pray about your answer, then create a plan to make any needed corrections.*

Tuesday   *York Station View*

Are not five sparrows sold for two pennies?
Yet not one of them is forgotten by God.

LUKE 12:6

*I*f you stand at the end of the platform at York Station, you can watch a constant succession of engine and train movement that, if you are a railway enthusiast, will fascinate you. But you will only be able to form a rough idea of the overall plan.

If, however, you are privileged to be taken into the magnificent electrical signal box that lies across platforms seven and eight, you will see a diagram of the entire track layout for five miles on either side of the station. At once you can look at the situation through the eyes of those who control it. You will see why this train is diverted from its normal running line and that one parked temporarily in a siding.

Some people feel that if they were really walking close to God, so that he could impart wisdom to them freely, then they would find themselves in the York Station signal box. We might suppose that the gift of wisdom consists in an ability to see why God has done what he has done in a particular case and to see what he is going to do next. But in truth this view would be more than our human minds could comprehend. God gives us the view that we need—from the end of the platform.

Reflect: *How does your life resemble an uninformed view of York Station? Do you resent that? Should you?*

Wednesday

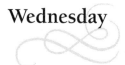

Wisdom's Inability

*The secret things belong
to the LORD our God.*

DEUTERONOMY 29:29

*I*f only we could discern the real purpose of everything that happens to us! Then it would be clear to us every moment how God was making all things work together for good. Christians suffering from depression—physical, mental, or spiritual (note, these are three different things!)—may drive themselves almost crazy with this kind of futile inquiry. For it *is* futile—make no mistake about that.

It is true that God has given us guidance by application of principles and that he will on occasion confirm it to us by unusual providences, which we will recognize at once as corroborative signs. But this is quite a different thing from trying to read a message about God's secret purposes out of every unusual thing that happens to us. So, far from the gift of wisdom consisting in the power to do this, the gift actually presupposes our conscious inability to do it.

Reflect: *How content are you with wisdom's inability?*

Thursday

Wise Driving

*I will give you a wise and
discerning heart.*

1 KINGS 3:12

*W*hat does it mean for God to give us wisdom? What kind of gift is it?

God-given wisdom is like being taught to drive. What matters in driving is the speed and appropriateness of your reactions to things and the soundness of your judgment as to what scope a situation gives you. You do not ask yourself why the road should narrow or screw itself into a dogleg wiggle just where it does, nor why that van should be parked where it is, nor why the driver in front should hug the crown of the road so lovingly. You simply try to see and do the right thing in the actual situation that presents itself.

To live wisely, you have to be clear-sighted and realistic—ruthlessly so—in looking at life as it is. The effect of divine wisdom is to enable you and me to do just that in the actual situations of everyday life.

Reflect: *What do you need to know and not know in order to drive well? How does this compare to wise living? What do you find encouraging (or frustrating) about this comparison?*

Friday

Meaningless

"Meaningless! Meaningless!"
says the Teacher.
"Utterly meaningless!
Everything is meaningless."

ECCLESIASTES 1:2

*E*cclesiastes" means simply "the preacher," and the book is a sermon. "Meaningless! Meaningless!" says the Teacher. "Utterly meaningless! Everything is meaningless." The author speaks as a mature teacher giving a young disciple the fruits of his own long experience and reflection (Ecclesiastes 11:9). He wants to lead his young believer into true wisdom.

Apparently the young man (like many since) was inclined to equate wisdom with wide knowledge and to suppose that one gains wisdom simply by assiduous book work (Ecclesiastes 12:12). Clearly, he took it for granted that wisdom, when he gained it, would tell him the reasons for God's various doings in the ordinary course of providence. What the preacher wants to show him is that the real basis of wisdom is a frank acknowledgment that this world's course is enigmatic, that much of what happens is quite inexplicable to us, and that most occurrences "under the sun" bear no outward sign of a rational, moral God ordering them.

Journal: *Begin a paragraph with the words, "Everything is meaningless." Then write your own continuation. As you write, be honest with yourself and with God.*

Saturday/Sunday   *Inscrutable*

> *No one can comprehend what goes on under the sun. Despite all his efforts to search it out, man cannot discover its meaning. Even if a wise man claims he knows, he cannot really comprehend it.*

ECCLESIASTES 8:17

*E*cclesiastes is intended as a warning against a misconceived quest for understanding.

Look (says the preacher) at the sort of world we live in. What do you see? You see life's background set by aimlessly recurring cycles in nature (Ecclesiastes 1:4-7). You see its shape fixed by times and circumstances over which we have no control (3:1-8). You see death coming to everyone sooner or later, but its coming bears no relation to whether it is deserved (7:15). The wicked prosper; the good don't (8:14).

Seeing all this, you realize that God's ordering of events is inscrutable. Much as you want to make it out, you cannot do so (8:17). The harder you try to understand the divine purpose in the ordinary providential course of events, the more obsessed you grow with the apparent aimlessness of everything and the more you are tempted to conclude that life really is as pointless as it looks.

Pray: *Admit to God your inability to fully understand his purposes. Ask him for relief from any pointless feelings about life.*

Monday   *Realistic Pessimism*

With much wisdom comes much sorrow;
the more knowledge, the more grief.

Ecclesiastes 1:18

*I*f life is senseless, then it is valueless. And in that case, what use is it working to create things, to build a business, to make money, even to seek wisdom, for none of this can do you any obvious good (Ecclesiastes 2:15-16, 22-23; 5:11)? It is to this pessimistic conclusion, says the preacher of Ecclesiastes, that optimistic expectations of finding the divine purpose of everything will ultimately lead you (1:17-18). And of course he is right. For the world we live in is in fact the sort of place that he has described. The God who rules it hides himself. Rarely does this world look as if a beneficent Providence were running it. Rarely does it appear that there is a rational power behind it at all. Often what is worthless survives, while what is valuable perishes.

Be realistic, says the preacher. Face the facts. See life as it is. You will have no true wisdom till you do. And then praise God for giving your life the meaning that the world does not hold.

Reflect: *Do you agree with the worldview described above? Why or why not?*

Tuesday

Spiritual Inertia

As you do not know the path of the wind . . . so you cannot understand the work of God, the Maker of all things.

*A*mong the seven deadly sins of medieval lore was sloth (*acedia*)—a hard-bitten, joyless apathy of spirit. There is a lot of it around today in Christian circles. The symptoms are personal spiritual inertia combined with critical cynicism about the churches and supercilious resentment of other Christians' initiative and enterprise. Behind this morbid and deadening condition often lies the wounded pride of one who thought he knew all about the ways of God in providence and then was made to learn by bitter and bewildering experience that he didn't.

This is what happens when we do not heed the message of Ecclesiastes. For the truth is that God in his wisdom, to make and keep us humble and to teach us to walk by faith, has hidden from us almost everything that we would like to know about the providential purposes that he is working out in the churches and in our own lives.

Pray: *Have you ever entered a time of spiritual inertia? Was it connected to expecting to know more of God's providence than is possible? If appropriate, confess and ask help in forsaking this deadly sin.*

Wednesday   *Wisdom Is . . .*

When times are good, be happy;
but when times are bad, consider:
God has made the one as well as the other.

ECCLESIASTES 7:14

$\mathcal{U}$p to this point, the preacher has helped us to see what wisdom is not. Does he give us any guidance as to what it is? Indeed he does. "Fear God and keep his commandments" (Ecclesiastes 12:13). Trust and obey him, reverence him, worship him, be humble before him, and never say more than you mean when you pray to him (5:1-7). Do good (3:12). Remember that God will someday take account of you (11:9), so eschew, even in secret, things that you will be ashamed of when they come to light before God (12:14). Live in the present, and enjoy it thoroughly (9:7-10). Seek grace to work hard at whatever life calls you to do (9:10), and enjoy your work as you do it (2:24). Leave to God its issues; let him measure its ultimate worth. Your part is to use all the good sense and enterprise at your command in exploiting the opportunities that lie before you (11:1-6).

Journal: *Read each passage outlined above and create a journal page from your findings. Begin: "Wisdom is . . ."*

Thursday   *The Way of Wisdom*

> *Trust in the LORD with all your heart*
> *and lean not on your own understanding.*

*T*his is the way of wisdom. We can be sure that the God who made this marvelously complex world order, who compassed the great redemption from Egypt, and who later compassed the even greater redemption from sin and Satan, knows what he is doing, and "doeth all things well," even if for the moment he hides his hand. We can trust him and rejoice in him, even when we cannot discern his path. Thus the preacher's way of wisdom boils down to what was expressed by Richard Baxter:

> Ye saints, who toil below, adore your heavenly King.
> And onward as ye go some joyful anthem sing.
> Take what He gives, and praise Him still
> Through good and ill who ever lives.

Journal: *Page back through your studies of wisdom. Like Richard Baxter, write your own song about true wisdom.*

Friday

Wisdom's Gifts

To the only wise God be glory
forever through Jesus Christ! Amen.

ROMANS 16:27

*W*isdom consists of choosing the best means to the best end. God's work of giving wisdom is a means to his chosen end of restoring and perfecting the relationship between himself and human beings—the relationship for which he made them. For what is this wisdom that he gives? It is not a sharing of all his knowledge but a disposition to confess that he is wise and to cleave to him and live for him in the light of this Word through thick and thin. Thus the effect of his gift of wisdom is to make us more humble, more joyful, more godly, more quick-sighted as to his will, more resolute in the doing of it, and less troubled (not less sensitive but less bewildered) than we were at the dark and painful things of which our life in this fallen world is full.

Pray: *Wisdom is not a sharing of all of God's knowledge but a disposition to confess that he is wise. In prayer, make this sort of confession, giving to God "the dark and painful things" of your life. Ask for the gifts of trust described above.*

Saturday/Sunday   *Wisdom's Fruit*

*Wisdom that comes from heaven
is first of all pure; then peace-loving,
considerate, submissive, full of mercy
and good fruit, impartial and sincere.*

JAMES 3:17

$\mathcal{T}$he New Testament tells us that the fruit of wisdom is Christlikeness—peace, humility, and love (James 3:17)—and the root of it is faith in Christ (1 Corinthians 3:18) as the manifested wisdom of God (1 Corinthians 1:30). Thus the kind of wisdom that God waits to give to those who ask him is a wisdom that will bind us to himself, a wisdom that will find expression in a spirit of faith and a life of faithfulness. Let us see to it, then, that our own quest for wisdom takes the form of a quest for these things and that we do not frustrate the wise purpose of God by neglecting faith and faithfulness in order to pursue a kind of knowledge that in this world is not given to us to have.

Journal: *List one of the eight fruits of wisdom from James 3:17 on each of the next eight days of your calendar. Look for opportunities to live out that particular aspect of Christlike wisdom during each day. Journal the results.*

SUMMER

Monday

God as King

Sanctify them by the truth;
your word is truth.

JOHN 17:17

*T*wo facts about the triune Jehovah are assumed in every biblical passage. The first is that he is *king*—absolute monarch of the universe, ordering all its affairs, working out his will in all that happens within it. The second fact is that he *speaks,* uttering words that express his will in order to cause it to be done.

A king in the ancient world would, in the ordinary course of things, speak for two purposes. On the one hand, he would enact regulations and laws that directly determine the environment—judicial, fiscal, cultural—within which his subjects must henceforth live. On the other hand, he would make a personal link between himself and his subjects. The Bible pictures the Word of God as having a similar twofold character.

God is the King. We, his creatures, are his subjects. His Word relates both to things around us and to us directly; God speaks both to determine our environment and to engage our minds and hearts.

Reflect: *In what ways is your relationship with God similar to people living under an ancient king? What kind of king is God? Write as many adjectives as you can.*

Tuesday

God's Invitation

You know when I sit and when I rise;
you perceive my thoughts from afar.

PSALM 139:2

*L*ike any king, God's word to us is not only of government but also of fellowship. For, though God is a great king, it is not his wish to live at a distance from his subjects. Rather the reverse: he made us with the intention that he and we might walk together forever in a love relationship.

But such a relationship can exist only when we know each other. God, our Maker, knows all about us before we say anything (Psalm 139:1-4), but we can know nothing about him unless he tells us. Here, therefore, is a further reason why God speaks to us: not only to move us to do what he wants but also to enable us to know him so that we may love him.

Therefore God sends his word to us in the character of both information and invitation. It comes to woo us as well as to instruct us. It does not merely put us in the picture of what God has done and is doing but also calls us into personal communion with the loving Lord himself.

Reflect: *In the presence of the God who knows you, read aloud the first four verses of Psalm 139—and respond as God leads you.*

Wednesday  *God Said*

God said, "Let us make man in
our image, in our likeness."

GENESIS 1:26

We meet the word of God in its various relations in the first three chapters of the Bible.

Look first at the story of Genesis 1. Verse 3 tells us how, amid chaos and sterility, "God said, 'Let there be light.'" What happened? Immediately "there was light." Seven more times God's creative word "Let there be . . ." was spoken, and step by step things sprang into being and order.

But then the story carries us on a further stage. God speaks to the man and woman whom he has made. "God . . . said to them . . ." (verse 28). Here is God addressing human beings directly. Thus fellowship between God and them is inaugurated.

Within the compass of these three short chapters we see the word of God in all relations in which it stands to the world and to man within it. On the one hand, it fixes man's circumstances and environment; on the other, it commands man's obedience, inviting his trust and opening to him the mind of the Maker.

Reflect: *Read the first three chapters of Genesis, seeking to know the mind of the Maker.*

Thursday

God-Touched Mouth

*The LORD reached out his hand and
touched my mouth and said to me, "Now,
I have put my words in your mouth."*

JEREMIAH 1:9

*T*hat the word of God really determines world events was the
first lesson God taught Jeremiah when he called him to be a
prophet. "See," God told him, "today I appoint you over nations
and kingdoms to uproot and tear down, to destroy and over-
throw, to build and to plant" (Jeremiah 1:10).

But how could this be? Jeremiah's call was not to be a
statesman but to be a prophet, God's messenger boy (1:7). How
could a man with no official position, whose only job was to talk,
be described as the God-appointed ruler of nations? Why, simply
because he had the words of the Lord in his mouth (verse 9), and
any word that God gave him to speak about the destiny of nations would certainly be fulfilled.

To fix this in Jeremiah's mind, God gave him his first vision.
God asked, "Jeremiah, what do you see?"

"A rod of almond."

"You have seen well, for I am watching over my word to
perform it" (Jeremiah 1:11-12 RSV).

Journal: *Whose mouth (or pages) has God used to draw you to
himself?*

Friday

Law, Promise, Testimony

*This is the one I esteem: he who is
humble and contrite in spirit,
and trembles at my word.*

ISAIAH 66:2

The Bible consistently presents the word of God as coming directly to us in the threefold character with which it was spoken in the Garden of Eden. Sometimes it comes as *law*—as at Sinai, in many sermons of the prophets, in much of Christ's teaching, and in the evangelical command to repent (Acts 17:30) and believe on the Lord Jesus Christ (1 John 3:23). Sometimes it comes as *promise*—as in the covenant promise given to Abraham (Genesis 17:1-8), the promises of the Messiah (Isaiah 11:1-2), and the New Testament promises of justification, resurrection, and glorification for believers. Sometimes, again, it comes as *testimony*—divine instruction concerning the facts of faith and the principles of piety, in the form of historical narration, theological argument, psalmody, and wisdom. Always it is stressed that the claim of the Word of God on us is absolute: the Word is to be received, trusted, and obeyed because it is the word of God the King.

Journal: *God's Word is law, promise, testimony. Journal Scripture passages that have become each of these for you.*

Saturday/Sunday   *Saints and Brutes*

You are near, O Lord,
and all your commands are true.

Psalm 119:151

*O*ur bodies are like machines, needing the right routine of food, rest, and exercise if they are to run efficiently. And they are liable, if filled up with the wrong fuel (alcohol, drugs, poison), to lose their power of healthy functioning and ultimately to "seize up" entirely in physical death.

God wishes us to think of our souls in a similar way. We were made to bear God's moral image. That is, our souls were made to "run" on the practice of worship, law keeping, truthfulness, honesty, discipline, self-control, and service to God and our fellows. If we abandon these practices, not only do we incur guilt before God, we also progressively destroy our own souls. Conscience atrophies; the sense of shame dries up; one's capacity for truthfulness, loyalty, and honesty is eaten away; one's character disintegrates. One not only becomes desperately miserable; one is steadily dehumanized. This is one aspect of spiritual death. Richard Baxter was right to formulate the alternatives as "a Saint—or a Brute." Everyone, sooner or later, consciously or unconsciously opts for one or the other.

Reflect: *Saint or brute: who have you seen as one or the other?*

Week Twenty-Eight

Monday   *God's Faithfulness*

Your faithfulness [reaches] to the skies.

Psalm 36:5

*T*he Bible proclaims God's faithfulness in superlative terms.
"Your faithfulness [reaches] to the skies." How does God's faithfulness show itself? By his unfailing fulfillment of his promises.
He is a covenant-keeping God who never fails those who trust
his word. Abraham proved God's faithfulness, waiting through a
quarter century of old age for the birth of his promised heir. Millions more have proved it since.

In the days when the Bible was universally acknowledged in
the churches as "God's Word written," it was clearly understood
that the way to strengthen one's faith was to focus it on particular
promises that spoke to one's condition. People sneer today at the
promise boxes that our grandparents used, but this attitude is
not a wise one. The promise boxes may have been open to abuse,
but the approach to Scripture and to prayer that they expressed
was right. It is something we have lost and need to recover.

Reflect: *Read God's promises below, then choose one for reflection and prayer: Isaiah 40:31; Isaiah 49:15-16; 1 Corinthians
15:51-56; 2 Corinthians 12:9; James 1:5; 1 Peter 3:12; 1 John 1:9;
Revelation 21:3-4.*

Tuesday

Christian Captives

*Oh, that my ways were steadfast
in obeying your decrees!*

PSALM 119:5

What is a Christian? Christians are people who acknowledge and live under the Word of God. Their eyes are on the God of the Bible as their Father and the Christ of the Bible as their Savior. Their consciences, like Luther's, are captive to the Word of God, and they aspire, like the psalmist, to have their whole lives brought into line with it. The promises of Scripture are before them as they pray, and the precepts are before them as they go about their daily tasks. In addition, Christians know that God's Word has gone forth to create and control and order things around them, but this thought brings them only joy. Christians are independent folks, for they use the Word of God as a touchstone by which to test the various views that are put to them, and they will not touch anything that they are not sure that Scripture sanctions.

Why does this description fit so few of us who profess to be Christians in these days? You'll find it profitable to ask your conscience and let it tell you.

Reflect: *Prayerfully conduct a "conscience check," using the paragraphs above as a guide.*

Wednesday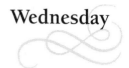

Love

God is love.

1 JOHN 4:8

$\mathcal{S}$t. John's twice-repeated statement "God is love" (1 John 4:8, 16) is one of the most tremendous utterances in the Bible—and also one of the most misunderstood. Yet the hard thought involved is more than repaid when the true sense of these texts comes home to the Christian soul. Those who climb Scotland's Ben Nevis do not complain of their labor once they see the view from the top!

To know God's love is indeed heaven on earth. And the New Testament sets forth this knowledge not as the privilege of a favored few but as a normal part of ordinary Christian experience. When Paul says, "the love of God is shed abroad in our hearts by the Holy Ghost which is given unto us" (Romans 5:5 KJV), he means not love for God, as Augustine thought, but knowledge of God's love for us. And though he had never met the Roman Christians to whom he was writing, he took it for granted that the statement would be as true of them as it was of him.

Journal: *"God is love." Journal a page of what you think this means and implies.*

Thursday

Flood of Love

*The love of God is shed abroad in
our hearts by the Holy Ghost
which is given unto us.*

ROMANS 5:5 KJV

Three points in Paul's words to the Romans deserve comment.

First, notice the verb "shed abroad." It means literally "poured (or dumped) out." It is the word used of the "outpouring" of the Spirit himself.

Second, notice that the instilling of this knowledge is described as part of the regular ministry of the Spirit to those who receive him—to all, that is, who are born again, all who are true believers.

Then, third, notice the tense of the verb. It is in the perfect tense, which implies a settled state consequent on a completed action. The thought is that knowledge of the love of God, having flooded our hearts, *fills them now*, just as a valley once flooded remains full of water. Paul assumes that all his readers, like himself, will be living in the enjoyment of a strong and abiding sense of God's love for them.

Pray: *Thank God for the love that he has flooded into your being.*

Friday   *Holy Ground*

*May you be strong to grasp, with all God's
people, what is the breadth and length and
height and depth of the love of Christ, and to
know it, though it is beyond knowledge.*

EPHESIANS 3:18-19 NEB

*R*evival means the work of God restoring to a moribund
church, in a manner out of the ordinary, those standards of
Christian life and experience that the New Testament sets forth
as being entirely ordinary. This includes a longing that the Spirit
may shed God's love abroad in our hearts with greater power. It
is with this (to which deep exercise of the soul about sin is often
preliminary) that personal revival begins, and it is by this that
revival in the church, once begun, is sustained.

In earlier devotionals, when we looked at God's wisdom, we
saw something of his mind. When we thought of his power, we
saw something of his hand and his arm. When we considered his
word, we learned about his mouth. But now, contemplating his
love, we are to look into his heart.

We will stand on holy ground. We need the grace of reverence,
that we may tread it without sin.

Reflect: *How can you express reverence for God's love?*

Saturday/Sunday *Love and Judgment*

> *I am the Lord, who exercises kindness,*
> *justice and righteousness on earth.*

> JEREMIAH 9:24

*G*od is love" is not the complete truth about God so far as the Bible is concerned. It is not an abstract definition that stands alone but a summing up, from the believer's standpoint, of what the whole revelation set forth in Scripture tells us about the Author. The God of whom John is speaking is the God who made the world, who judged it by the flood, who called Abraham and made of him a nation, who chastened his Old Testament people by conquest, captivity, and exile, who sent his Son to save the world, who cast off unbelieving Israel and (shortly before John wrote) destroyed Jerusalem, and who would one day judge the world in righteousness. It is this God, says John, who is love. It is not possible to argue that a God who is love cannot also be a God who condemns and punishes the disobedient.

Reflect: *Reflect on the last sentence above. How do you put together God's love and his judgment?*

Monday

Spirit

God is spirit.

John 4:24 RSV

*S*pirit" contrasts with "flesh." Christ's point is that while we, being flesh, can be present in only one place at a time, God, being spirit, is not so limited. God is nonmaterial, noncorporeal, and therefore nonlocalized.

The first of the Anglican Thirty-Nine Articles further brings out the meaning of God's "spirituality" (as the books call it) by the rather odd-sounding assertion that he is "without body, parts, or passions." Something very positive is being expressed by these negations. The love of the God who is spirit is no fitful, fluctuating thing, as human love is, nor is it a mere impotent longing for things that may never be. It is, rather, a spontaneous determination of God's whole being in an attitude of benevolence and benefaction, an attitude freely chosen and firmly fixed.

There are no inconstancies or vicissitudes in the love of almighty God, who is spirit. Nothing can separate from God's love those whom it has once embraced.

Journal: *Read Romans 8:35-39. Then write a prayer of response to God.*

Tuesday

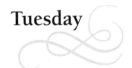

Light

*God is light; in him there
is no darkness at all.*

1 JOHN 1:5

*G*od is light." Those who "walk in the light," seeking to be like God in holiness and righteousness of life and eschewing everything inconsistent with this, enjoy fellowship with the Father and the Son. Those who "walk in the darkness," whatever they may claim for themselves, are strangers to this relationship (1 John 1:6-7). So the God who is love is first and foremost light, and sentimental ideals of his love as an indulgent, benevolent softness, divorced from moral standards and concerns, must therefore be ruled out from the start.

God's love is holy love. The God whom Jesus made known is not a God who is indifferent to moral distinctions but a God who loves righteousness and hates iniquity, a God whose ideal for his children is that they should "be perfect . . . as your heavenly Father is perfect" (Matthew 5:48). He will not take into his company any person, however orthodox in mind, who will not follow after holiness of life.

Reflect: *Do you more naturally tend toward "holiness in mind" or "holiness of life"? How can you become more of each and therefore "walk in the light"?*

Wed-nesday   *All Things?*

*We know that in all things God works for
the good of those who love him, who have
been called according to his purpose.*

"God is love" is the complete truth about God as far as the
Christian is concerned. God's love finds expression in everything
that he says and does. This is a supreme comfort for Christians.
As believers, we find in the cross of Christ assurance that we, as
individuals, are beloved of God. Knowing this, we are able to
apply to ourselves the promise that all things work together for
good. Not just *some* things, note, but *all* things! Thus, so far as
we are concerned, God is love to us—holy, omnipotent love—at
every moment and in every event of everyday life. Even when we
cannot see the why and the wherefore of God's dealings, we
know that there is love in and behind them, and so we can rejoice
always, even when, humanly speaking, things are going wrong.
We know that the true story of our life, when known, will prove
to be, as the old hymn says, "mercy from first to last"—and we
are content.

Pray: *What do you find difficult to accept in the paragraph above?
Talk to God about it.*

Thursday

Goodness

The LORD is good to all;
he has compassion on all he has made.

PSALM 145:9

*G*od's love is an exercise of his goodness. The Bible means by God's goodness his cosmic generosity. Goodness in God, writes Louis Berkhof, is "that perfection of God which prompts him to deal bountifully and kindly with all His creatures. It is the affection which the Creator feels towards His sentient creatures as such."

Of this goodness, God's love is the supreme and most glorious manifestation. "Love, generally," wrote James Orr, "is that principle which leads one moral being to desire and delight in another, and reaches its highest form in that personal fellowship in which each lives in the life of the other, and finds his joy in imparting himself to the other, and in receiving back the outflow of that other's affection unto himself." Such is the love of God.

Journal: *Meditate on the first sentence above. Then journal some of your own experiences with God's love expressed in his goodness.*

Friday

Love Unevoked

This is love: not that we loved God,
but that he loved us and sent his Son
as an atoning sacrifice for our sins.

1 JOHN 4:10

God's love is an exercise of his goodness toward sinners. As such, it has the nature of grace and mercy. It is a kindness that is not merely undeserved but is actually contrary to desert, for the objects of God's love are rational creatures who have broken God's law, whose natures are corrupt in God's sight, and who merit only condemnation and final banishment from his presence.

It is staggering that God should love sinners, yet it is true. God loves creatures who have become unlovely and (one would have thought) unlovable. There was nothing whatever in the objects of his love to call it forth. Love among persons is awakened by something in the beloved, but the love of God is free, spontaneous, unevoked, uncaused. God loves people because he has chosen to love them—as Charles Wesley put it, "he hath loved us, because he would love"—and no reason for his love can be given except his own sovereign good pleasure.

Journal: *To paraphrase Charles Wesley, "He hath loved me—because he would love." Journal your response to God.*

Saturday/Sunday

Chosen

> *He chose us in him before the*
> *creation of the world to be holy*
> *and blameless in his sight.*

EPHESIANS 1:4

*G*od's love is an exercise of his goodness toward individuals. God's purpose of love, formed before creation, involved, first, the choice and selection of those whom he would bless and, second, the appointment of the benefits to be given them and the means whereby these benefits would be procured and enjoyed. All this was made sure from the start. So Paul writes to the Thessalonian Christians, "We are bound to give thanks to God always for you, brethren *beloved by the Lord,* because God chose you [selection] from the beginning [before creation] to be saved [the appointed end], through sanctification by the Spirit and belief in the truth [the appointed means]" (2 Thessalonians 2:13 RSV).

The exercise of God's love toward individual sinners in time is the execution of his purpose to bless those same individual sinners—a purpose that he formed in eternity.

Reflect: *Meditate, phrase by phrase, on Ephesians 1:4. What does it say about God? about you? about love? Pray your response to God.*

Monday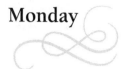

God's Singing

The LORD your God is with you. . . .
He will rejoice over you with singing.

ZEPHANIAH 3:17

*I*f a father continues cheerful and carefree while his son is getting into trouble, we wonder at once how much love there can be in their relationship, for we know that those who truly love are happy only when those whom they love are truly happy also. So it is with God in his love for us. God's happiness is not complete till all his beloved ones are finally out of trouble—in William Cowper's words,

> Till all the ransomed church of God
> Be saved to sin no more.

God has set his love on particular sinners, and he will not know perfect and unmixed happiness again till he has brought every one of them to heaven. Thus God saves not only for his glory but also for his gladness. The thought passes understanding and almost beggars belief, but there is no doubt that, according to Scripture, such is the love of God.

Reflect: *Read Zephaniah 3:17, placing yourself within this vivid image of God's love. Bring these thoughts to mind throughout the coming day.*

Tuesday 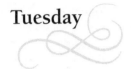 *God's Gift*

> *God demonstrates his own love*
> *for us in this: While we were still*
> *sinners, Christ died for us.*

> ROMANS 5:8

*G*od's love to sinners was expressed by the gift of his Son to be their Savior. The measure of love is how much it gives, and the measure of the love of God is the gift of his only Son to become human and to die for sins and so to become the one mediator who can bring us to God. Was there ever such costly munificence?

New Testament writers constantly point to the cross of Christ as the crowning proof of the reality and boundlessness of God's love. Thus John goes straight on from his first "God is love" to say, "This is how God showed his love among us: He sent his one and only Son into the world that we might live through him. This is love: not that we love God, but that he loved us and sent his Son as an atoning sacrifice for our sins" (1 John 4:9-10).

Pray: *Offer your personal thanks for God's gift, an expression of his love.*

Wednesday

Abraham's Heirs

If you belong to Christ, then you are Abraham's seed, and heirs according to the promise.

GALATIANS 3:29

*G*od's love to sinners brings them to know and enjoy him in a covenant relation. A covenant relation is one in which two parties are permanently pledged to each other in mutual service and dependence (example: marriage).

Biblical religion has the form of a covenant relation with God. The first occasion on which the terms of the relation were made plain was when God showed himself to Abraham as El Shaddai (God Almighty, God All-Sufficient) and formally gave him the covenant promise "to be your God and the God of your descendants after you" (Genesis 17:7). All Christians inherit this promise through faith in Christ, as Paul argues in Galatians 3:15-29.

"This is true love to any one," said John Tillotson, "to do the best for him we can." This is what God does for those he loves—the best he can. And the measure of the best that God can do is omnipotence! Thus faith in Christ introduces us into incalculable blessing, both now and for eternity.

Reflect: *Page through the book of Genesis, pausing to read some of the story of Abraham and his descendants. Sense your connection (through Christ) to these deep roots of your family tree.*

Thursday

Love Lived

Dear friends, since God so loved us,
we also ought to love one another.

1 JOHN 4:11

*I*s it true that God is love to me as a Christian? If so, certain questions arise. Why do I ever grumble and show discontent and resentment at the circumstances in which God has placed me? Why am I ever distrustful, fearful, or depressed? Why do I ever allow myself to grow cool, formal, and halfhearted in the service of the God who loves me so? Why do I ever allow my loyalties to be divided so that God has not all my heart?

John wrote that "God is love" in order to make an ethical point: "Since God so loved us, we also ought to love one another." Could an observer learn from the quality and degree of love that I show to others—my spouse, my family, my neighbors, people at church, people at work—anything at all about the greatness of God's love to me?

Let us examine ourselves.

Pray: *Select three questions above and meditate on them. Give honest answers regarding your thoughts and motives. Ask God's help for any needed changes to your heart.*

Friday

Grace

*Paul and Barnabas . . . talked
with them and urged them to
continue in the grace of God.*

ACTS 13:43

*I*t is commonplace in all the churches to call Christianity a religion of grace. It is a truism of Christian scholarship that grace is a personal activity, God operating in love toward people. It is a staple diet in the Sunday school that grace is "God's Riches at Christ's Expense." And yet, despite these facts, there do not seem to be many in our churches who actually believe in grace. Talk to them about the church's heating or last year's accounts, and they are with you at once. But speak to them about the realities to which the word *grace* points, and their attitude is one of deferential blankness. They do not accuse you of talking nonsense. They do not doubt that your words have meaning. But they feel that, whatever it is you are talking about, it is beyond them, and the longer they have lived without it, the surer they are that at their stage of life they do not really need it.

Reflect: *To what extent are the concerns addressed above true in your own church? What can you do about it?*

Saturday/Sunday   *Pagan Thinking*

> *The heart is deceitful above all things,*
> *and desperately wicked: who can know it?*

JEREMIAH 17:9 KJV

*W*e tend to have too high an opinion of ourselves. We dismiss a bad conscience, in ourselves as in others, as an unhealthy psychological freak, a sign of disease and mental aberration rather than an index of moral reality. We are convinced that, despite all our little peccadilloes—drinking, gambling, reckless driving, sexual laxity, lies, sharp practice in trading, dirty reading and viewing, and what have you—we are at heart thoroughly good folks. Then, as pagans do (and the modern human heart is pagan—make no mistake about that), we imagine God as a magnified image of ourselves and assume that God shares our own complacency about ourselves. The thought of ourselves as creatures fallen from God's image, rebels against God's rule, guilty and unclean in God's sight, fit only for God's condemnation, never enters our heads. And without this understanding of sin, we miss our desperate need for grace.

Reflect: *When are you tempted to engage in this "pagan" type of thinking?*

Monday

Zero Tolerance

*Will not the Judge of all
the earth do right?*

GENESIS 18:25

$\mathcal{T}$he retributive justice of God points to grace. In our pagan way, we take it for granted that God tolerates sin as we do. The idea that retribution might be the moral law of God's world and an expression of his holy character seems to us quite fantastic. Yet the Bible insists throughout that the world that God in his goodness has made is a moral world, one in which retribution is as basic a fact as breathing. God is the Judge of all the earth, and God is not true to himself unless he punishes sin. Unless one knows and feels the truth of this fact that wrongdoers have no natural hope of anything from God but retributive judgment, one can never share the biblical faith in divine grace.

Reflect: *Retribution means that people get what they deserve. Why might you find this comforting? Why might you also find it worrisome?*

Tuesday  *Thou Alone*

No one will be declared righteous in [God's] sight by observing the law.

ROMANS 3:20

*A*ncient pagans tried to entice the gods to give favors by multiplying gifts and sacrifices to them. Modern pagans seek to do it by churchmanship and morality. Conceding that they are not perfect, they still have no doubt that respectability henceforth will guarantee God's acceptance of them in the end, whatever they may have done in the past. But the Bible's position is as expressed in Augustus Toplady's hymn "Rock of Ages."

Not the labours of my hand can fulfill Thy law's demands.
Could my zeal no respite know, could my tears forever flow.
All for sin could not atone.

This leads to the admission of one's own helplessness and to the conclusion:

Thou must save, and Thou alone.

To mend our own relationship with God is beyond the power of any of us. And one must see and bow to this truth before one can share the biblical faith in God's grace.

Pray: *Find the entire text of Augustus Toplady's hymn "Rock of Ages." Meditate on each line of the song, then read aloud all four verses as your own prayer.*

Wednesday

No Obligations

*[God] is not served by human hands,
as if he needed anything.*

ACTS 17:25

The sovereign freedom of God points us to grace.

Modern paganism has at the back of its mind a feeling that God is somehow obliged to love and help us, little though we deserve it. This was the feeling voiced by the French freethinker who died muttering, "God will forgive—that's his job." But this feeling is not well founded.

The God of the Bible does not depend on his human creatures for his well-being. We can claim from him only justice. He is not obliged to pity and pardon. If he does so, it is an act done, as we say, "of his own free will." Nobody forces his hand.

Grace is free, in the senses of being self-originated and of proceeding from One who was free not to be gracious. Only when it is seen that what decides each individual's destiny is whether or not God resolves to save him from his sins—and that this is a decision that God need not make in any single case—can one begin to grasp the biblical view of grace.

Reflect: *"Grace is free." What does that statement mean as it reflects God's nature?*

Thursday

God's Fountain

On that day a fountain will be opened . . .
to cleanse them from sin and impurity.

ZECHARIAH 13:1

*T*he grace of God is love freely shown toward guilty sinners, contrary to their merit and indeed in defiance of their demerit. We have to ask, why should this thought mean so much? Once a person is convinced that his state and need are as the New Testament describes, the gospel of grace cannot but sweep him off his feet with wonder and joy. For it tells how our Judge has become our Savior. As Isaac Watts put it:

> But there's a voice of princely grace sounds from God's
> holy Word;
> Ho! Ye poor captive sinners, come, and trust upon the Lord.
> To the blest fountain of thy blood, incarnate God, I fly,
> To wash my soul from scarlet stains, and sins of deepest dye.

People who can sincerely take Watts's words on their lips will not soon tire of singing the praises of grace.

Journal: *Write your own praise of God's grace.*

Friday   *Pardoning Grace*

He who did not spare his own Son, but gave him up for us all—how will he not also, along with him, graciously give us all things?

ROMANS 8:32

$\mathcal{J}$ustification is the truly dramatic transition from the status of a condemned criminal awaiting a terrible sentence to that of an heir awaiting a fabulous inheritance. Justification is by faith; it takes place the moment a person puts vital trust in the Lord Jesus Christ as Savior. Justification is free to us, but it was costly to God, for its price was the atoning death of God's Son. Why was it that God "did not spare his own Son, but gave him up for us all"? Because of his grace.

The reaction of the Christian heart contemplating all this was given supreme expression by the one-time president of Princeton, Samuel Davies:

In wonder lost, with trembling joy, we take the pardon of
    our God;
Pardon for crimes of deepest dye, a pardon bought with
    Jesus' blood:
Who is a pardoning God like Thee? Or who has grace so
    rich and free?

Reflect: *What impact does God's pardoning grace have on you?*

Saturday/Sunday   *God's Great Plan*

*In him we have redemption through
his blood, the forgiveness of sins,
in accordance with the riches of
God's grace that he lavished on us.*

EPHESIANS 1:7-8

*P*ardon is the heart of the gospel, but it is not the whole doctrine of grace. For the New Testament sets God's gift of pardon in the context of a plan of salvation that began with election before the world was made and will be completed only when the church is perfect in glory. Its fullest account is in the massive paragraph running from Ephesians 1:3 to 2:10.

Well might Isaac Watts cry, in words as magnificent as they are true:

Engraved as in eternal brass the mighty promise shines;
Nor can the powers of darkness rase those everlasting lines.
His very word of grace is strong as that which built the skies
The voice that rolls the stars along speaks all the promises.

The stars indeed may fall, but God's promises will stand and be fulfilled. The plan of salvation will be brought to a triumphant completion. Thus grace will be shown to be sovereign.

Journal: *Study Ephesians 1:3–2:10. Create an outline, phrase by phrase, that shows the flow of God's great plan of salvation.*

Monday 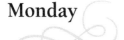 *Saints Preserved*

> *Those God foreknew he also*
> *predestined to be conformed to the*
> *likeness of his Son, that he might be*
> *the firstborn among many brothers.*

ROMANS 8:29

*G*race is the guarantee of the preservation of the saints. If the plan of salvation is certain of accomplishment, then the Christian's future is assured. I am, and will be, "kept by the power of God through faith unto salvation" (1 Peter 1:5 KJV). I need not torment myself with the fear that my faith may fail. As grace led me to faith in the first place, so grace will keep me believing to the end.

Faith, both in its origin and its continuance, is a gift of grace. So the Christian may sing along with the hymn,

> Grace first inscribed my name, in God's eternal book;
> 'Twas grace that gave me to the Lamb who all my
>   sorrows took.
> Grace taught my soul to pray, and pardoning love to know;
> 'Twas grace that kept me to this day, and will not let me go.

Journal: *Copy the words of Romans 8:29 and the hymn above, personalizing them by writing your own name into the text. Reflect on the place God has given you in his eternal plan.*

Tuesday

Grace and Gratitude

We are God's workmanship, created in Christ Jesus to do good works, which God prepared in advance for us to do.

EPHESIANS 2:10

It has been said that in the New Testament doctrine is grace and ethics is gratitude. Something is wrong with any form of Christianity in which, experimentally and practically, this saying is not being verified. For love awakens love in return, and love, once awakened, desires to give pleasure.

The revealed will of God is that those who have received grace should henceforth give themselves to good works. And gratitude will move anyone who has truly received grace to do as God requires and daily to cry out thus—

Oh! To grace how great a debtor daily I'm constrained to be;
Let that grace now, like a fetter, bind my wandering heart
   to Thee!
Prone to wander, Lord, I feel it; prone to leave the God
   I love—
Here's my heart, oh, take and seal it, seal it for Thy
   courts above!

Reflect: *As part of his grace to you, God has already prepared good works for you to do (Ephesians 2:8-10). How have you seen this taking place in your life thus far? How can you be alert to tasks God has given for the current phase of your life?*

Wednesday   *God the Judge*

God will judge men's secrets through
Jesus Christ, as my gospel declares.

ROMANS 2:16

*D*o you believe in divine judgment? By which I mean, do you believe in a God who acts as your Judge? Many, it seems, do not. But there are few things stressed more strongly in the Bible than the reality of God's work as Judge.

People who do not actually read the Bible confidently assure us that when we move from the Old Testament to the New the theme of divine judgment fades into the background. But if we examine the New Testament, even in the most cursory way, we find at once that the Old Testament emphasis on God's action as Judge, far from being reduced, is actually intensified. The entire New Testament is overshadowed by the certainty of a coming day of universal judgment and by the problem thence arising: How may we sinners get right while there is yet time? From the New Testament we also learn that Jesus is the world's Judge—its Savior as well.

Reflect: *Savior and Judge in the same person. What would this mean in a human court? What does it mean spiritually that Jesus is both Savior and Judge?*

Thursday

Giving Account

*They will have to give account
to him [God] who is ready to judge
the living and the dead.*

1 PETER 4:5

What is involved in the idea of the Father or Jesus being a judge? Four thoughts at least are involved.

First, God the Judge is a person with authority. As our Maker, he owns us, and as our Owner, he has a right to dispose of us. He is both the Lawgiver and the Judge.

Second, God the Judge is a person identified with what is good and right. The Bible leaves us in no doubt that God loves righteousness and hates iniquity and that the ideal of a judge wholly identified with what is good and right is perfectly fulfilled in him.

Third, God the Judge is a person of wisdom, to discern truth. When the Bible pictures God judging, it emphasizes his omniscience and wisdom as the searcher of hearts and the finder of facts. He knows us, and judges us, as we really are.

Last, God the Judge is a person of power to execute sentences. God is his own executioner. As he legislates and sentences, so he punishes. All judicial functions coalesce in him.

Pray: *Recognizing that God our Judge is all that is described above and more, bring to him in prayer all that you are and all that you hope to become.*

Friday   *The Heart of Justice*

> *We must all appear before the judgment seat*
> *of Christ, that each one may receive what is*
> *due him for the things done while in the body,*
> *whether good or bad.*

2 CORINTHIANS 5:10

The Bible's proclamation of God's work as Judge is part of its witness to his character. It shows us that the heart of the justice that expresses God's nature is retribution (the rendering to persons what they have deserved), for this is the essence of the judge's task. To reward good with good, and evil with evil, is natural to God. The retributive principle applies throughout: Christians as well as non-Christians will receive according to their works. Retribution is the inescapable moral law of creation. God will see that each person sooner or later receives what they deserve—if not here, then hereafter. This is one of the basic facts of life. And, being made in God's image, we all know in our hearts that this is *right*. This is how it ought to be.

Journal: *What is your predominant feeling about God's judgment: anticipation or dread? Why?*

Saturday/Sunday

The Just Judge

God "will give to each person
according to what he has done."

*W*e often wonder if there is justice in this world. But the character of God is the guarantee that all wrongs will be righted someday. God is the Judge, so justice will be done. Why then do we fight the thought of God as Judge?

The truth is that part of God's moral perfection is his perfection in judgment. Would a God who did not care about the difference between right and wrong be a good and admirable Being? Would a God who put no distinction between the beasts of history, the Hitlers and Stalins (if we dare use names), and his own saints be morally praiseworthy and perfect? Moral indifference would be an imperfection in God, not a perfection. Not to judge the world would be to show moral indifference. The final proof that God is a perfect moral Being, not indifferent to questions of right and wrong, is the fact that he has committed himself to judge the world.

Pray: *As you read today's news, pause now and then to thank God that he will someday bring justice.*

Monday   *God's Triumph*

> *Fear God and keep his commandments,*
> *for this is the whole duty of man. For*
> *God will bring every deed into judgment.*

ECCLESIASTES 12:13-14

*I*t is clear that the reality of divine judgment must have a direct effect on our view of life. If we know that retributive judgment faces us at the end of the road, we will not live as we otherwise would. But it must be emphasized that the doctrine of divine judgment, and particularly of the final judgment, is not to be thought of primarily as a bogey with which to frighten men into an outward form of conventional "righteousness." True, it has its frightening implications for godless men, but its main thrust is a revelation of the moral character of God and an imparting of moral significance to human life. As Leon Morris has written, "The Christian view of judgment means that history moves to a goal. . . . Judgment protects the idea of the triumph of God and of good."

Reflect: *What purpose does God's judgment give to you in a personal sense? In a global sense?*

Tuesday   *The End of the Road*

> *When the Son of Man comes in his glory, . . .*
> *he will sit on his throne . . . and he will*
> *separate the people one from another as a*
> *shepherd separates the sheep from the goats.*

MATTHEW 25:31-32

The Anglican burial service addresses Jesus in a single breath as "holy and merciful Savior, thou most worthy Judge eternal."

Jesus constantly affirmed that in the day when all appear before God's throne to receive the abiding and eternal consequences of the life they have lived, he himself will be the Father's agent in judgment, and his word of acceptance or rejection will be decisive. "A time is coming when all who are in their graves will hear his voice and come out—those who have done good will rise to live, and those who have done evil will rise to be condemned" (John 5:28-29). Jesus stands at the end of life's road for everyone.

"Prepare to meet your God" was Amos's message to Israel (Amos 4:12). "Prepare to meet the risen Jesus" is God's message to the world today (see Acts 17:31). And we can be sure that he who is true God and perfect man will make a perfectly just judge.

Reflect: *What do you look forward to in the scene described above?*

Wednesday
Heart Index

*Out of the overflow of the
heart the mouth speaks.*

MATTHEW 12:34

*F*inal judgment will be according to our works, that is, our "doings," our whole course of life. The relevance of our doings is not that they ever merit an award from the court—they fall too far short of perfection to do that—but that they provide an index of what is in the heart.

Jesus once said, "Men will have to give account on the day of judgment for every careless word they have spoken. For by your words you will be acquitted, and by your words you will be condemned" (Matthew 12:36-37). What is the significance of the words we utter (utterance is, of course, a "work" in the relevant sense)? Just this: the words show what you are inside.

It is not that one way of acting is meritorious while the other is not, but from these actions it can be seen whether there is love for Christ, the love that springs from faith, in the heart (see Matthew 25:34-46).

Journal: *When has God used someone's words for your spiritual benefit? Write a prayer of thanks to God. If it is appropriate, also write your thanks to this person.*

Thursday

No Condemnation

> *There is therefore now no condemnation*
> *for those who are in Christ Jesus.*

ROMANS 8:1

*P*aul refers to the fact that we must all appear before Christ's judgment seat as "the terror of the Lord" (2 Corinthians 5:11 KJV), and well he might. Jesus the Lord, like his Father, is holy and pure; we are neither. We live under his eye, he knows our secrets, and on judgment day the whole of our past life will be played back before him and brought under review. If we know ourselves at all, we know we are not fit to face him. What are we to do?

As Judge, Christ is the law. But as Savior, he is the gospel. So call on the coming Judge to be your present Savior. You will then discover that you are looking forward to that future meeting with joy. Says Augustus M. Toplady:

> While I draw this fleeting breath; when my eyelids close
> in death;
> When I soar through tracts unknown, see thee on thy
> judgment-throne;
> Rock of Ages, cleft for me, let me hide myself in thee.

Reflect: *When you consider Jesus as both your coming Judge and present Savior, how does your future hope impact your present life?*

Friday   *God's Wrath*

*God remembered Babylon the Great
and gave her the cup filled with the
wine of the fury of his wrath.*

REVELATION 16:19

*W*rath is an Old English word defined as "deep, intense anger, and indignation." And wrath, the Bible tells us, is an attribute of God.

How often during the past year did you hear—or, if you are a minister, did you preach—a sermon on the wrath of God? How long is it, I wonder, since a Christian spoke straight on this subject on radio or television? (And if one did so, how long would it be before that person would be asked to speak again?) The fact is that the subject of divine wrath has become taboo in our society, and Christians by and large have accepted that taboo.

One cannot imagine that talk of divine judgment was ever very popular, yet the biblical writers engage in it constantly. As A. W. Pink said, "There are *more* references in Scripture to the anger, fury, and wrath of God, than there are to His love and tenderness." God is good to those who trust him and terrible to those who do not.

Journal: *List several questions you have not yet resolved about the wrath of God.*

Saturday/Sunday   *Righteous Indignation*

God is a righteous judge, a God who expresses his wrath every day.

PSALM 7:11

*G*od's love, as the Bible views it, never leads him to foolish, impulsive, immoral actions in the way that its human counterpart too often leads us. And in the same way, God's wrath in the Bible is never the capricious, self-indulgent, irritable, ignoble thing that human anger so often is. It is, instead, a right and necessary reaction to objective moral evil. God is angry only where anger is called for. Even among humans, there is such a thing as righteous indignation, though it is perhaps rarely found. But all God's indignation is righteous.

Would a God who took as much pleasure in evil as he did in good be a good God? Would a God who did not react adversely to evil in this world be morally perfect? Surely not. But it is precisely this adverse reaction to evil, which is a necessary part of moral perfection, that the Bible has in view when it speaks of God's wrath. We can trust God's wrath just as we can trust God's love.

Journal: *Attempt to write a definition of "righteous indignation" for a Christian and for God. How might you know if your own indignation is righteous?*

Monday

The Weight of Sin

Will [God] not repay each person
according to what he has done?

PROVERBS 24:12

*G*od's wrath in the Bible is always judicial. That is, it is the wrath of the Judge administering justice. God's wrath is that each receives precisely what he or she deserves. To quote Jonathan Edwards in his sermon "Sinners in the Hands of an Angry God," God our Judge will see "that you shall not suffer beyond what strict justice requires." But it is precisely "what strict justice requires," Edwards insists, that will be so grievous for those who die in unbelief.

It may be asked, can disobedience to our Creator really deserve great and grievous punishment? Anyone who has ever been convicted of sin knows beyond any shadow of doubt that the answer is yes. Such a person knows too that those whose consciences have not yet been awakened to consider, as Anselm put it, "how weighty is sin" are not yet qualified to give an opinion.

Pray: *In prayer, bring to God someone you fear will fall into the hands of an "angry God" because of his or her unrepented sin.*

Tuesday   *God Gave Them Over*

> *God gave them over in the sinful*
> *desires of their hearts . . . to shameful*
> *lusts . . . to a depraved mind.*

ROMANS 1:24, 26, 28

*R*omans shows the revelation of God's wrath. To those who have eyes to see, tokens of the active wrath of God appear here and now in the actual state of humankind. Everywhere the Christian observes a pattern of degeneration constantly working itself out—from knowledge of God to worship of that which is not God, and from idolatry to immorality of an ever grosser sort so that each generation grows a fresh crop of ungodliness and unrighteousness. In this decline we are to recognize the present action of divine wrath in a process of judicial hardening and withdrawal of restraints, whereby people are given up to their own corrupt preferences and so come to put into practice more and more uninhibitedly the lusts of their sinful hearts. Paul describes the process with the key phrase "God gave them over . . ." The gospel prepares us for its good news by telling us the bad news of a coming "day of wrath and revelation of the righteous judgment of God" (Romans 2:5 KJV).

Reflect: *From the perspective of a person hardened to sin, what does "God gave them over" look like? What does it look like from an eternal perspective?*

Wednesday

Divine Deliverance

[We are] justified freely by his grace through the redemption that is in Christ Jesus: Whom God hath set forth to be a propitiation through faith in his blood.

ROMANS 3:24-25 KJV

$\mathcal{R}$omans shows our deliverance from God's wrath. It is through the blood of Jesus Christ, the incarnate Son of God. And what does it mean to be "justified"? It means to be forgiven and accepted as righteous. And how do we come to be justified? Through faith, that is, self-abandoning trust in the person and work of Jesus. And how does Jesus' blood—that is, his sacrificial death—form a basis for our justification? Paul explains this in Romans 3:24-25. Propitiation means a sacrifice that averts wrath through expiating sin and canceling guilt.

Between us sinners and the thunderclouds of divine wrath stands the cross of the Lord Jesus. If we are Christ's, through faith, then we are justified through his cross, and the wrath will never touch us, neither here nor hereafter. Jesus "delivers us from the wrath to come" (1 Thessalonians 1:10 RSV).

Journal: *"Justified," "redemption," "propitiation." Write a brief definition of each, along with its personal impact on you. Create a prayer of thanks using all three words.*

Thursday

Fire Snatchers

Beloved, . . . save some, by
snatching them out of the fire.

JUDE 20, 23 RSV

*N*o doubt it is true that the subject of divine wrath has in the past been handled speculatively, irreverently, even malevolently. No doubt there have been some who have preached of wrath and damnation with tearless eyes and no pain in their hearts. No doubt the sight of small sects cheerfully consigning the whole world, apart from themselves, to hell has disgusted many. Yet if we would know God, it is vital that we face the truth concerning his wrath, however strong our initial prejudices against it. Otherwise we will not understand the gospel of salvation from wrath nor the wonder of the redeeming love of God. Nor will we understand the hand of God in history and God's present dealings with our own people. Nor will we be able to make heads or tails of the book of Revelation. Nor will our evangelism have the urgency enjoined by Jude—"save some, by snatching them out of the fire" (Jude 23 RSV).

Reflect: *Reflect on your own status as "beloved" by Christ. How might that status encourage you to try to snatch someone you know from the fire of God's wrath?*

Friday

Goodness and Severity

*Behold . . . the goodness
and severity of God.*

ROMANS 11:22 KJV

$\mathcal{B}$ehold therefore the goodness and severity of God," writes Paul in Romans. The critical word here is "and."

The apostle is explaining the relation between Jew and Gentile in the plan of God. He has just reminded his Gentile readers that God rejected the great mass of their Jewish contemporaries for unbelief while at the same time bringing many pagans like themselves to saving faith. Now he invites them to take note of the two sides of God's character that appeared in this transaction. "Behold therefore the goodness and severity of God: on them which fell, severity; but toward thee, goodness" (Romans 11:22 KJV). The Christians at Rome are not to dwell on God's goodness alone, nor on his severity alone, but to contemplate both together.

Both are attributes of God—aspects, that is, of his revealed character. Both appear alongside each other in the economy of grace. Both must be acknowledged together if God is to be truly known.

Journal: *Goodness and severity are both attributes of God. Write several questions that come to mind as you contemplate these qualities joined together in his nature.*

Saturday/Sunday   *God Is Good*

> *The LORD said, "I will cause all my goodness*
> *to pass in front of you, and I will proclaim my*
> *name, the LORD, in your presence."*

EXODUS 33:19

*W*hen the biblical writers call God "good," they are thinking in general of all those moral qualities that prompt his people to call him perfect. And they are thinking in particular of the generosity that moves them to call him merciful and gracious and to speak of his love. When God stood with Moses on Sinai, what he said was this: "The LORD, the LORD, the compassionate and gracious God, slow to anger, abounding in love and faithfulness, maintaining love to thousands, and forgiving wickedness, rebellion and sin" (Exodus 34:6-7). All the particular perfections that are mentioned here, and all that go with them (God's truthfulness and trustworthiness; his unfailing justice and wisdom; his tenderness, forbearance, and entire adequacy to all who penitently seek his help; his noble kindness in offering believers the exalted destiny of fellowship with him in holiness and love) together make up God's goodness in the sense of the sum total of his revealed excellences.

Pray: *Create a list of all God's goodnesses mentioned above, then pray a prayer of praise based on that list.*

Monday

God's Severity

*God's kindness leads you
toward repentance.*

ROMANS 2:4

*W*hat, now, of God's severity? The word Paul uses in Romans 11:22 for "sternness" means literally "cutting off." It denotes God's decisive withdrawal of his goodness from those who have spurned it. The principle that Paul is applying here is that behind every display of divine goodness stands a threat of severity in judgment if that goodness is scorned. Earlier in Romans, Paul addressed the self-satisfied non-Christian critic of human nature as follows: "God's kindness *leads you* toward repentance." Similarly, Paul tells the Roman Christians that God's goodness is their portion only on a certain condition—"provided that you continue in his kindness. Otherwise, you also will be cut off" (Romans 11:22).

But God is not impatient in his severity; just the reverse. He is "slow to anger" (Nehemiah 9:17 KJV) and "longsuffering" (Exodus 34:6 KJV). The patience of God in giving a chance to repent before judgment finally falls (Revelation 2:5) is one of the marvels of the Bible story. It is no wonder that the New Testament stresses that to be longsuffering is a Christian virtue and duty. It is, in truth, a part of the image of God.

Reflect: *Are you more likely to repent because of kindness or severity?*

Tuesday

Payback

How can I repay the LORD for
all his goodness to me?

PSALM 116:12

*H*ow can we respond to God's goodness and severity? By appreciating the goodness of God. Count your blessings. Learn not to take natural benefits, endowments, and pleasures for granted; learn to thank God for them all. Do not slight the Bible or the gospel of Jesus Christ by an attitude of casualness toward either. The Bible shows you a Savior who suffered and died in order that we sinners might be reconciled to God. Calvary is the measure of the goodness of God; lay it to heart.

How else can we respond? By appreciating the patience of God. Think how he has borne with you, and still bears with you, when so much in your life is unworthy of him and you have so richly deserved his rejection. Learn to marvel at his patience, and seek grace to imitate it in your dealings with others; try not to try his patience anymore. Ask yourself the psalmist's question—"How can I repay the LORD for all his goodness to me?" Seek God's grace to give you your answer.

Journal: *Write your own response to the question of Psalm 116:12.*

Wednesday

Discipline

*My son, do not make light
of the Lord's discipline.*

HEBREWS 12:5

*H*ow can we respond to God's goodness and severity? By appreciating the discipline of God.

All things come from God, and you have tasted his goodness every day of your life. Has this experience led you to repentance and faith in Christ? If not, you are trifling with God and stand under the threat of his severity. But if he (in George Whitefield's phrase) puts thorns in your bed, it is only to awaken you from the sleep of spiritual death. If you are a true believer and he still puts thorns in your bed, it is only to keep you from falling into the somnolence of complacency and to let your sense of need bring you back constantly to him.

This kindly discipline, in which God's severity touches us for a moment in the context of his goodness, is meant to keep us from having to bear the full brunt of that severity apart from that context. It is a discipline of love, and it must be received accordingly. "It was good for me to be afflicted so that I might learn your decrees" (Psalm 119:71).

Journal: *What events of your past could cause you to say the words of Psalm 119:71?*

Thursday

Jealousy

I, the LORD your God, am a jealous God.

EXODUS 20:5

A jealous God"—doesn't it sound offensive? For we know jealousy, the green-eyed monster, as a vice—one of the most cancerous and soul-destroying vices—whereas God, we are sure, is perfectly good. How, then, could anyone ever imagine that jealousy is found in him?

The first step in answering this question is to make it clear that this is not a case of imagining anything. Were we imagining a God, then naturally we should ascribe to him only characteristics that we admired, and jealously would not enter the picture. Nobody would imagine a jealous God. But we are not making up an idea of God by drawing on our imagination; we are seeking instead to listen to the words of Holy Scripture in which God tells us the truth about himself.

God our Creator has revealed himself. He has talked. He has spoken through many human agents and messengers and supremely through his Son, our Lord Jesus Christ. And there in the Bible—God's "public record," as John Calvin called it—we find God speaking repeatedly of his jealousy.

Journal: *Write a list of questions that come to your mind when you think of God as a jealous God.*

Friday

Consuming Fire

The LORD your God is a
consuming fire, a jealous God.

DEUTERONOMY 4:24

*W*hat is the nature of divine jealousy? How can jealousy be a virtue in God when it is a vice in humans? God's perfections are matter for praise, but how can we praise God for being jealous?

When faced with God's anthropomorphisms, it is easy to get hold of the wrong end of the stick. We have to remember that people are not the measure of their Maker and that when the language of human personal life is used of God, none of the limitations of human creaturehood are thereby implied.

Those elements in human qualities that show the corrupting effect of sin have no counterpart in God. Thus, for instance, his wrath is not the ignoble outburst that human anger so often is, a sign of pride and weakness, but it is holiness reacting to evil in a way that is morally right and glorious. In the same way, God's jealousy is not a compound of frustration, envy, and spite, as human jealousy so often is, but it appears instead as a (literally) praiseworthy zeal to preserve something supremely precious.

Reflect: *What differences do you see between human jealousy and God's jealousy?*

Saturday/Sunday   *Vicious Jealousy*

> *Anger is cruel and fury overwhelming,*
> *but who can stand before jealousy?*

PROVERBS 27:4

*V*icious human jealousy is an expression of the attitude "I want what you've got, and I hate you because I haven't got it." It is an infantile resentment springing from unmortified covetousness, which expresses itself in envy, malice, and meanness of action. It is terribly potent, for it feeds and is fed by pride, the taproot of our fallen nature. There is a mad obsessiveness about jealousy that, if indulged, can tear an otherwise firm character to shreds. What is often called sexual jealousy, the lunatic fury of a rejected or supplanted suitor, is of this kind. "Who can stand before jealousy?" asks the wise man of Proverbs 27.

Journal: *Gregory the Great saw pride as "the beginning of all sin" and thus the taproot leading to the kind of jealousy described above. Sinful jealousy and its root sin of pride are both sins of the mind; they rarely show to others—and sometimes not to ourselves. For three days, keep a spiritual log, making a note whenever jealousy enters your mind. At the end of three days, notice any connections to pride, then confess your sins to God.*

Monday

Good Jealousy

Are we trying to arouse the Lord's jealousy?
Are we stronger than he?

1 CORINTHIANS 10:22

*N*ot all jealousy is evil. There is a righteous sort of human jealousy—a zeal to protect a love relationship. It appears not as the blind reaction of wounded pride but as the fruit of marital affection. This sort of jealousy is a positive virtue, for it shows a grasp of the true meaning of the husband-wife relationship together with a proper zeal to keep it intact.

Scripture consistently views God's jealousy as being of this latter kind. That is, his jealousy is an aspect of his covenant love for his own people. The Old Testament regards God's covenant as his marriage with Israel, carrying with it a demand for unqualified love and loyalty. The worship of idols, and all compromising relations with non-Israelite idolaters, constituted disobedience and unfaithfulness, which God saw as spiritual adultery, provoking him to jealousy and vengeance.

God demands utter and absolute loyalty from those whom he has loved and redeemed, and he will vindicate his claim by stern action against them if they betray his love by unfaithfulness.

Pray: *Give thanks to God for his covenant relationship with you and his jealous guarding of that love.*

Tuesday

Jealous Zeal

The zeal of the Lord Almighty
will accomplish this.

Isaiah 9:7

*G*od's jealousy over his people presupposes his covenant love, and this love is no transitory affection, accidental and aimless, but is the expression of a sovereign purpose. The goal of the covenant love of God is that he should have a people on earth as long as history lasts and after that should have all his faithful ones of every age with him in glory. And it is in the light of God's overall plan for his world that his jealousy must, in the last analysis, be understood. For God's ultimate objective is threefold: (1) to vindicate his rule and righteousness by showing his sovereignty in judgment on sins, (2) to ransom and redeem his chosen people, and (3) to be loved and praised by them for his glorious acts of love and self-vindication.

God seeks what we should seek—his glory, in and through people. And it is for the securing of this end, ultimately, that he is jealous. His jealousy, in all its manifestations, is precisely "the zeal of the Lord Almighty" for fulfilling his own purpose of justice and mercy.

Reflect: *Read Isaiah 9:6-7, meditating on each phrase. What will God's jealous zeal accomplish?*

Wednesday

The Name of God

Thus saith the Lord GOD; . . .
[I] will be jealous for my holy name.

EZEKIEL 39:25 KJV

*G*od's jealousy leads him, on the one hand, to judge and destroy the faithless among his people who fall into idolatry and sin (Joshua 24:19-20) and indeed to judge the enemies of righteousness and mercy everywhere (Nahum 1:2). It also leads him, on the other hand, to restore his people after national judgment has chastened and humbled them (Zechariah 1:14-17). And what is it that motivates these actions? Simply the fact that he is "jealous for [his] holy name" (Ezekiel 39:25 KJV).

God's "name" is his nature and character as Jehovah, the Lord, ruler of history, guardian of righteousness, and savior of sinners. And God means his name to be known, honored, and praised. "I am the LORD; that is my name! I will not give my glory to another or my praise to idols" (Isaiah 42:8). "For my own sake, I do this. How can I let myself be defamed? I will not yield my glory to another" (Isaiah 48:11). Here in these texts is the quintessence of the jealousy of God.

Reflect: *"God means his name to be known, honored, and praised."*
What is your part in this mission?

Thursday

Begin to Begin

The zeal of thine house hath eaten me up.

JOHN 2:17 KJV

*T*he jealousy of God requires us to be zealous for God. As our right response to God's love for us is love for him, so our right response to his jealousy over us is zeal for him. His concern for us is great; ours for him must be great too.

The second commandment implies that God's people should be positively and passionately devoted to God's person, his cause, and his honor. The Bible word for such devotion is *zeal,* sometimes actually called "jealousy for God." God himself, as we have seen, manifests this zeal, and the godly must manifest it too.

Does zeal for the house of God and the cause of God eat us up? possess us? consume us? Can we say with the Master, "My food is to do the will of him who sent me and to finish his work" (John 4:34)? What sort of discipleship is ours? Have we not the need to pray with that flaming evangelist George Whitefield (a man as humble as he was zealous), "Lord, help me to begin to begin"?

Pray: *Page back through the past seven studies on God's jealousy, then pray George Whitefield's prayer as your own.*

Friday

Spit Out

> *Because you are lukewarm—*
> *neither hot nor cold—I am about*
> *to spit you out of my mouth. . . .*
> *Be [zealous], and repent.*

REVELATION 3:16, 19

*T*he jealousy of God threatens churches that are not zealous for God.

We love our churches. They have hallowed associations. We cannot imagine them displeasing God, at any rate not seriously. But the Lord Jesus once sent a message to a church very much like some of ours—the complacent church of Laodicea—in which he told the Laodicean congregation that their lack of zeal was a source of supreme offense to him. Anything would be better than self-satisfied apathy! "So then because thou art lukewarm, and neither cold nor hot, *I will spue thee out of my mouth. . . . Be zealous* therefore, and repent" (Revelation 3:16, 19 KJV).

How many of our churches today are sound, respectable—and lukewarm? What, then, must Christ's word be to them? What have we to hope for unless, by the mercy of the God who in wrath remembers mercy, we find zeal to repent?

Revive us, Lord, before judgment falls!

Pray: *Consider ways your own church might fit the description above—and pray for her.*

Saturday/Sunday   *What Is a Christian?*

> *To all who received him, to those
> who believed in his name, he gave the
> right to become children of God.*

JOHN 1:12

*W*hat is a Christian? The richest answer I know is that a Christian is one who has God as Father. But cannot this be said of every person, Christian or not? Emphatically no! The idea that all are children of God is not found in the Bible anywhere. The Old Testament shows God as the Father not of all but of his own people, the seed of Abraham. The New Testament has a world vision, but it shows God as the Father not of all but of those who put their trust in the Lord Jesus Christ as their divine sin-bearer and so become Abraham's spiritual seed. Sonship to God is not, therefore, a universal status into which everyone enters by natural birth but rather is a supernatural gift that one receives through receiving Jesus. The gift of sonship to God becomes ours not through being born but through being born again: "To all who received him."

Journal: *Spend five minutes writing as many names as you can from any era who are (to the best of your knowledge) children of God. Thank God for your connection to each one through the generosity of his adoption.*

Monday   *Adopted*

*How great is the love the Father
has lavished on us, that we should
be called children of God!*

1 JOHN 3:1

$\mathcal{S}$onship to God is a gift of grace. It is not a natural but an adoptive sonship, and so the New Testament explicitly pictures it. In Roman law it was a recognized practice for an adult who wanted an heir, and someone to carry on the family name, to adopt a male as his son—usually at age, rather than in infancy as is the common way today. The apostles proclaim that God has so loved those whom he redeemed on the cross that he has adopted them all as his heirs, to see and share the glory into which his only begotten Son has already come. "God sent his Son . . . to redeem those under law, that we might receive the full [adoptive] rights of sons" (Galatians 4:4-5). This refers to those who were "foreordained unto adoption as sons of Jesus Christ unto himself" (Ephesians 1:5 RV). "How great is the love the Father has lavished on us!"

Reflect: *What does it mean that God's love is "lavish"? How have you experienced that kind of love given to you?*

Tuesday

> *[God] said, "I am the God of your father, the God of Abraham, the God of Isaac and the God of Jacob." At this, Moses hid his face, because he was afraid to look at God.*

> EXODUS 3:6

*O*ur understanding of Christianity cannot be better than our grasp of adoption. The revelation to the believer that God is his Father is in a sense the climax of the Bible.

In Old Testament times, God gave his people a covenant name by which to speak of him and call on him: the name Yahweh ("Jehovah," "the LORD"). By this name, God announced himself as the great "I AM," the One who is completely and consistently himself. He *is,* and it is because he is what he is that everything else is as it is. That name proclaimed God as self-existent, sovereign, and wholly free from constraint by, or dependence on, anything outside himself.

Though Yahweh was his covenant name, it spoke to Israel of what their God was *in himself* rather than of what he would be in relation to them. It was the official name of Israel's King, and there was something of regal reserve about it. It was an enigmatic name, a name calculated to awaken humility and awe on the mystery of the divine.

Reflect: *Meditate on the concept that God, the great I AM, adopted you. Respond in prayer.*

Wednesday

Holy God

*Holy, holy, holy is the L*ORD *Almighty;*
the whole earth is full of his glory.

ISAIAH 6:3

$\mathcal{T}$he angels' song that Isaiah heard in the temple, with its emphatic repetitions ("Holy, holy, holy is the LORD Almighty"), could be used to characterize the whole Old Testament. The word *holy* expresses separation, or separateness. When God is declared to be holy, the thought is of all that separates him and sets him apart and makes him different from his creatures—his greatness and his purity. The whole spirit of Old Testament religion was determined by the thought of God's holiness. Sinful creatures must learn to humble themselves and be reverent before God. Religion was "the fear of the Lord"—a matter of knowing your own littleness, of confessing your faults and abasing yourself in God's presence, of sheltering thankfully under his promises of mercy, and of taking care, above all things, to avoid presumptuous sins. Again and again it was stressed that we must keep our place and our distance when in the presence of a holy God. This emphasis overshadowed everything else.

Journal: *Write a prayer that focuses on God's holiness and your own response to this aspect of his nature.*

Thursday   *Drawing Near*

*[Since] by a new and living way [Jesus]
opened for us through the curtain, . . .
let us draw near to God with a sincere
heart in full assurance of faith.*

HEBREWS 10:20, 22

*I*n the New Testament, the Old Testament revelation of the holiness of God and its demand for humility in humanity is presupposed. But something has been added. New Testament believers deal with God as their Father.

The stress of the New Testament is not on the difficulty and danger of drawing near to the holy God but on the boldness and confidence with which believers may approach him. This is a boldness that springs directly from faith in Christ and from the knowledge of his saving work. "In him and *through faith in him* we may approach God with freedom and confidence" (Ephesians 3:12). "Let us draw near to God with a sincere heart in full assurance of faith" (Hebrews 10:22).

To those who are Christ's, the holy God is a loving Father. They belong to his family. They may approach him without fear and always be sure of his fatherly concern and care. This is the heart of the New Testament message.

Journal: *Beside yesterday's entry, write another prayer, this time responding to God's invitation to "draw near."*

Friday

A father to the fatherless . . .
is God in his holy dwelling.

PSALM 68:5

I have heard it seriously argued that the thought of divine fatherhood can mean nothing to those whose human father was inadequate, lacking wisdom, affection, or both, nor to those many more whose misfortune it was to have a fatherless upbringing. And yet our Maker is our perfect parent—faithful in love and care, generous and thoughtful, interested in all we do, respecting our individuality, skillful in training us, wise in guidance, always available, helping us to find ourselves in maturity, integrity, and uprightness. Seeing God in this light can have meaning for everybody. It doesn't matter whether we come to it by saying, "I had a wonderful father, and I see that God is like that, only more so," or by saying, "My father disappointed me here and here, but God—praise his name—will be very different," or even by saying, "I have never known what it is to have a father on earth, but thank God I now have one in heaven."

Journal: *Journal a comparison between your human father (or lack of one) and God as your Father. How have your human-father experiences led you to value all that God is as your divine Father?*

Saturday/Sunday   *Divine Fatherhood*

*I kneel before the Father, from whom
his whole family in heaven and
on earth derives its name.*

EPHESIANS 3:14-15

*G*od has not left us to guess what his fatherhood amounts to
by drawing analogies from human fatherhood. He revealed the
full meaning of this relationship once and for all through our
Lord Jesus Christ, his own incarnate Son.

First, fatherhood implied *authority.* "I have come down from
heaven not to do my will but to do the will of him who sent me"
(John 6:38).

Second, fatherhood implied *affection.* "The Father loves the
Son" (John 5:20).

Third, fatherhood implied *fellowship.* "I am not alone, for my
Father is with me" (John 16:32).

Fourth, fatherhood implied *honor.* "The Father . . . has entrusted all judgment to the Son, that all may honor the Son just
as they honor the Father" (John 5:22-23).

All this extends to God's adopted children. In, through, and
under Jesus Christ their Lord, they are ruled, loved, companied
with, and honored by their heavenly Father.

Reflect: *How can the relationship between Jesus and his Father
help you relax as a child of the same Father?*

Monday 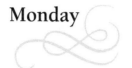 *Adoption Defined*

You received the Spirit of sonship.
And by him we cry, "Abba, Father."

ROMANS 8:15

$\mathcal{A}$ formal definition and analysis of what adoption means comes from the Westminster Confession (chapter twelve):

> All those that are justified, God vouchsafeth, in and for His only Son Jesus Christ, to make partakers of the grace of adoption: by which they are taken into the number, and enjoy the liberties and privileges of the children of God; have His name put upon them, receive the Spirit of adoption; have access to the throne of grace with boldness; are enabled to cry, Abba, Father; are pitied, protected, provided for, and chastened by Him, as by a father; yet never cast off, but sealed to the day of redemption, and inherit the promises, as heirs of everlasting salvation.

This is the nature of the divine sonship that is bestowed on believers.

Reflect: *What do you find in the definition from the Westminster Confession that helps you appreciate your adopted status in God's family? Talk to him about it in prayer.*

Tuesday   The Gift of Justification

> "Repent . . . and turn to God,
> so that your sins may be wiped out."

ACTS 3:19

*J*ustification is the gift of God on which, since Luther, evangelicals have laid the greatest stress. Justification (by which we mean God's forgiveness of the past, together with his acceptance for the future) is the primary and fundamental blessing of the gospel. It is the primary blessing because it meets our primary spiritual need.

Justification is a forensic idea, conceived in terms of law and viewing God as judge. We all stand by nature under God's judgment. His law condemns us. Guilt gnaws at us, making us restless, miserable, and, in our lucid moments, afraid. We have no peace in ourselves because we have no peace with our Maker.

So we need the forgiveness of our sins and assurance of a restored relationship with God more than we need anything else in the world. This the gospel offers us before it offers us anything else.

Reflect: *What does justification provide the Christian? If justification alone were to spell out your connection with God, what would you find missing?*

Wednesday   *Part of God's Family*

You are no longer a slave, but a son;
and since you are a son, God
has made you also an heir.

GALATIANS 4:7

*A*doption is the highest privilege that the gospel offers, higher even than justification. Justification is the primary, fundamental blessing, but adoption is higher because of the richer relationship with God that it involves. Adoption is a family idea, conceived in terms of love and viewing God as Father. In adoption, God takes us into his family and fellowship—he establishes us as his children and heirs. Closeness, affection, and generosity are at the heart of the relationship.

To be right with God the Judge is a great thing, but to be loved and cared for by God the Father is greater. Adoption is founded on a nearer, more tender, and more endearing relation—that between a Father and his son. So the privilege of adoption presupposes pardon and acceptance, but it is higher than either. "Behold, what manner of love the Father hath bestowed upon us, that we should be called the sons of God" (1 John 3:1 KJV).

Reflect: *"Behold, what manner of love . . ." Reflect on God's love for you, illustrated in both justification and adoption. Thank him for all that this brings to mind.*

Thursday

Born Again!

God sent forth his Son . . . to redeem
them that were under the law, that we
might receive the adoption of sons.

GALATIANS 4:4-5 KJV

We do not fully feel the wonder of the passage from death to life that takes place in the new birth till we see it as a transition into the "safety, certainty, and enjoyment" of the family of God.

When Charles Wesley found Christ in 1738, his experience overflowed into some marvelous verses.

> Where shall my wondering soul begin? How shall I all to
> heaven aspire?
> A slave redeemed from death and sin, a brand plucked
> from eternal fire,
> How shall I equal triumphs raise, or sing my great
> Deliverer's praise?
> O how shall I the goodness tell, Father, which thou to me
> hast showed?
> That I, a child of wrath and hell, I should be called a
> child of God.

Three days later, Charles tells us in his diary, brother John burst in with "a troop of our friends" to announce that he too was now a believer, and "we sang the hymn with great joy."

Reflect: *Make Wesley's words your own, as if you could reach back over the centuries and sing with them that jubilant celebration of new birth.*

Friday

Abide

Abide in me, and I in you.

JOHN 15:4 KJV

*A*doption is a blessing that abides. A family unit needs to be stable and secure, and any unsteadiness in the parent-child relationship takes its toll in the child himself. The depressions, randomnesses, and immaturities that sometimes mark the children of broken homes are known to us all. But things are not like that in God's family. There you have absolute stability and security. The Parent is entirely wise and good, and the child's position is permanently assured. The very concept of adoption is itself a proof and guarantee of the preservation of the saints, for only bad fathers throw their children out of the family, even under provocation, and God is not a bad Father but a good one.

When one sees depression, randomness, and immaturity in Christians, one cannot but wonder whether they have learned the health-giving habit of dwelling in the abiding security of true children of God.

Reflect: *Spend ten minutes in silent meditation as you reflect on all that your adoption as a child of God implies. Use those ten minutes to "abide" in Christ.*

Saturday/Sunday
Brothers

> *Both the one who makes men holy and*
> *those who are made holy are of the same family.*
> *So Jesus is not ashamed to call them brothers.*

HEBREWS 2:11

*T*he entire Christian life has to be understood in terms of adoption. All of our Lord's teaching on Christian discipleship is cast in these terms. Just as Jesus always thought of himself as Son of God in a unique sense, so he always thought of his followers as children of his heavenly Father, members of the same divine family as himself. Early in his ministry, we find him saying, "Whoever does God's will is my brother and sister and mother" (Mark 3:35). After his resurrection, he called his disciples his brothers. "Go . . . to my brothers and tell them, 'I am returning to my Father and your Father, to my God and your God'" (John 20:17). The writer to the Hebrews assures us that the Lord Jesus regards all those for whom he has died, and whom he makes into his disciples, as his brothers (Hebrews 2:11).

As our Maker is our Father, so our Savior is our brother when we come into the family of God.

Journal: *Write reflections on your spiritual connections with others in God's family.*

Monday 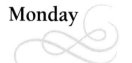 *Christian Conduct*

*Put on the new self, created to be like
God in true righteousness and holiness.*

EPHESIANS 4:24

*A*doption appears in the Sermon on the Mount as the basis of
Christian conduct. This sermon teaches Christian conduct, not
by giving a full scheme of rules and a detailed casuistry to be
followed with mechanical precision, but by indicating in a broad
and general way the spirit, direction, and objectives, the guiding
principles and ideals, by which the Christian must steer his
course. This is an ethic of responsible freedom, quite different
from the tax-consultant type of instruction that was the stock-
in-trade of Jewish lawyers and scribes in our Lord's day. That is
precisely the kind of moral instruction that good parents are
constantly trying to give their children—concrete and imaginative, teaching general principles from particular instances,
seeking all the time to bring the children to appreciate and share
the parents' own attitudes and view of life.

The reason why the Sermon has this quality is not far to seek.
It is because it is, in truth, instruction for children of a family—
God's family.

Reflect: *Read the Sermon on the Mount (Matthew 5–7), looking
for guidance in your own conduct.*

Tuesday

Father First

*Be imitators of God . . . as
dearly loved children.*

EPHESIANS 5:1

The Sermon on the Mount brings three all-embracing principles of conduct that our Lord lays down.

Number one is the principle of *imitating the Father.* The children must show the family likeness in their conduct. Jesus is here spelling out "Be holy, for I am holy"—and spelling it out in family terms.

Number two is the principle of *glorifying the Father.* "Let your light shine before men, that they may see your good deeds and praise your Father in heaven" (Matthew 5:16). Christians must seek to behave in public in a way that brings praise to their Father in heaven.

Number three is the principle of *pleasing the Father.* In Matthew 6:1-18, Jesus dwells on the need to be a single-minded God pleaser. The purpose of our Lord's promise of reward (6:4, 6, 18) is not to make us think in terms of wages but simply to remind us that our heavenly Father will notice and show special pleasure when we concentrate our efforts on pleasing him and him alone.

Journal: *Reread sections of the Sermon on the Mount (Matthew 5–7), and record one way you will challenge yourself to imitate the Father, glorify the Father, and please the Father.*

Wednesday

Cheeky Praying

If you, . . . though you are evil, know how to give good gifts to your children, how much more will your Father in heaven give good gifts to those who ask him!

MATTHEW 7:11

Adoption appears in the Sermon on the Mount as the basis of Christian prayer. As Jesus always prayed to his God as Father (*Abba* in Aramaic, an intimate family word), so must his followers do. The Father is always accessible to his children and is never too preoccupied to listen to what they have to say. This is the basis of Christian prayer.

Two things follow, according to the Sermon on the Mount. First, prayer must not be thought of in impersonal or mechanical terms, as a technique for putting pressure on someone who otherwise might disregard you. Second, prayer may be free and bold. We need not hesitate to imitate the sublime "cheek" of the child who is not afraid to ask his parents for anything because he knows he can count completely on their love. "Ask, and it will be given to you. . . . Everyone who asks receives" (Matthew 7:7-8).

Pray: *Experiment with "cheeky praying" to the Father who loves you, trusting him to do what is best.*

Thursday

Thorns and Grace

*Three times I pleaded with the Lord to
take it away from me. But he said to me,
"My grace is sufficient for you."*

2 CORINTHIANS 12:8-9

*O*ur Father in heaven does not always answer his children's prayers in the form in which we offer them. Sometimes we ask for the wrong thing! It is God's prerogative to give good things, things that we have need of, and if in our un-wisdom we ask for things that do not come under these headings, God, like any good parent, reserves the right to say, "No, not that; it wouldn't be good for you—but have this instead."

Good parents never simply ignore what their children are saying, nor simply disregard their feelings of need, and neither does God. But often he gives us what we should have asked for rather than what we actually requested. Paul asked the Lord Jesus graciously to remove his thorn in the flesh, and the Lord replied by graciously leaving it and strengthening Paul to live with it (2 Corinthians 12:7-9). The Lord knew best! To suggest that because Paul's prayer was answered this way it was not answered at all would be utterly wrong. Here is a source of much light on what is sometimes miscalled "the problem of unanswered prayer."

Journal: *Write about an experience when God did not answer your prayer as you had hoped. If you are able, express your trust that this "thorn" is accompanied by his grace.*

Friday

Basic Needs

Do not worry about your life,
what you will eat or drink;
or about your body,
what you will wear.

MATTHEW 6:25

*A*doption appears in the Sermon on the Mount as the basis of the life of faith, that is, the life of trusting God for one's material needs as one seeks his kingdom and righteousness. It is needless, I hope, to make the point that one can live the life of faith without forgoing gainful employment, though some are called to do this. But all Christians are called to a life of faith, in the sense of following God's will at whatever cost and trusting him for the consequences. And all are tempted, sooner or later, to put status and security, in human terms, before loyalty to God's call. Then, if they resist this temptation, they are at once tempted to worry about the likely effect of their stand, particularly when following Jesus has obliged them actually to forfeit some measure of security or prosperity that they could otherwise have expected to enjoy. On those thus tempted in the life of faith, Jesus brings the truth of their adoption to bear.

Reflect: *How can your adoption into God's family help you deal with the temptations described above?*

Saturday/Sunday   *Worry*

> *Look at the birds of the air; . . . your*
> *heavenly Father feeds them. Are you not*
> *much more valuable than they?*

> MATTHEW 6:26

*D*o not worry," says our Lord.

"But how can I help worrying," we ask, "when I face this and this and this?"

Jesus replies, "Your faith is too small. Have you forgotten that God is your Father? If God cares for the birds, whose Father he is not, is it not plain that he will certainly care for you, whose Father he is? 'Seek first his [your Father's] kingdom and his righteousness, and all these things will be given to you as well'" (Matthew 6:33).

"We might have a crash," said the small girl anxiously as the family car threaded its way through traffic.

"Trust Daddy; he's a good driver," said Mommy, and the young lady relaxed at once.

Do you trust your heavenly Father like that? If not, why not? Such trust is vital; it is the mainspring of the life of faith, without which it becomes a life of at least partial unbelief.

Pray: *Examine your current worries: "I do not trust God for . . ." Respectfully ask God to meet the need that worry reflects and also to increase your trust in his kind wisdom.*

FALL

Monday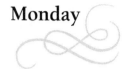

Great Love

Through Christ Jesus the law
of the Spirit of life set me free from
the law of sin and death.

ROMANS 8:2

*O*ur adoption shows us the greatness of God's love. The gift of pardon for the past is great:

Bearing shame and scoffing rude, in my place condemned
    he stood,
Sealed my pardon with his blood.

So, too, the gift of immunity and acceptance now and for the future is great:

No condemnation now I dread, Jesus, and all in him, is mine;
Alive in him, my living head, and clothed in
    righteousness divine,
Bold I approach the eternal throne
And claim the crown, through Christ my own.

Once Charles Wesley's ecstatic epitome of Romans 8 in "And Can It Be?" becomes yours, then your spirit takes wing and flies.

Reflect: *Read aloud all of Romans 8, taking joy in the greatness of God's adoptive love.*

Tuesday

Heirs

> *If we are [God's] children, then we are heirs—*
> *heirs of God and co-heirs with Christ.*

ROMANS 8:17

When you realize that God has taken you, a miraculously pardoned offender, and made you a child of his own house, then your sense of what Isaac Watts called God's "love beyond degree" is more than words can express. You will echo Charles Wesley's question:

> O how shall I the goodness tell,
> Father, which Thou to me has showed?
> That I, a child of wrath and hell,
> I should be called a child of God!

God adopts us out of free love, not because our character and record show us worthy to bear his name but despite the fact that they show the opposite. We are not fit for a place in God's family. The idea of his loving and exalting us sinners as he loves and has exalted the Lord Jesus sounds ludicrous and wild, yet that, and nothing less than that, is what our adoption means.

Journal: *Journal some of your ideas about what it means to be a coheir with Christ.*

Wednesday — *Eternity of Love*

I have loved you with an everlasting love;
I have drawn you with loving-kindness.

JEREMIAH 31:3

*A*doption, by its nature, is an art of free kindness to the person adopted. God adopts because he chooses to. Nor does his grace stop short with that initial act, any more than the love of human parents who adopt stops short with completing the legal process that makes the child theirs.

The establishing of the child's status as a member of the family is only a beginning. The real task remains: to establish a genuinely filial relationship between your adopted child and yourself. It is this, above all, that you want to see. Accordingly, you set yourself to win the child's love by loving the child. You seek to excite affection by showing affection.

So with God. Throughout our life in this world, and to all eternity beyond, he will constantly be showing us, in one way or another, more and more of his love, thereby increasing our love to him continually. The prospect before the adopted children of God is an eternity of love.

Pray: *Pray your response to a promised eternity of God's love.*

Thursday

Enduring Love

> *Give thanks to the LORD, for he is good.* His love endures forever.

PSALM 136:1

*O*nce I knew a family in which the eldest child was adopted at a time when the parents thought they could have no children. When their natural-born children arrived later on, they diverted all their affection to them, and the adopted eldest was left out in the cold. It was painful to see and, judging by the look on the eldest child's face, it was painful to experience. It was, of course, a miserable failure in parenthood.

But in God's family, things are not like that. God receives us as sons and daughters, and he loves us with the same steadfast affection with which he eternally loves his beloved Only Begotten. There are no distinctions of affection in the divine family. We are all loved just as fully as Jesus is loved.

It is like a fairy story—the reigning monarch adopts waifs and strays to make princes of them. But praise God, it is not a fairy story. It is hard and solid fact, founded on the bedrock of free and sovereign grace. This, and nothing less than this, is what adoption means.

Reflect: *Compare God's adoption of us with what is good about human adoptions.*

Friday

God's Children

The Spirit himself testifies with our spirit that we are God's children.

ROMANS 8:16

*N*ew Testament Christianity is a religion of hope, a faith that looks forward. For the Christian, the best is always yet to be. But how can we form any notion of that which awaits us at the end of the road? Here too the doctrine of adoption comes to our help.

To start with, it teaches us to think of our hope not as a possibility, nor yet as a likelihood, but as a guaranteed certainty, because it is a promised inheritance. The reason for adopting, in the first-century world, was specifically to have an heir to whom one could bequeath one's goods. So, too, God's adoption of us makes us his heirs and so guarantees to us, as our right (we might say), the inheritance that he has in store for us. "We are God's children."

Our Father's wealth is immeasurable, and we are to inherit the entire estate.

Journal: *"We are to inherit the entire estate." Journal what might be included in that "estate." Give thanks to God.*

Saturday/Sunday

Liberation

*Creation itself will be liberated
from its bondage to decay.*

ROMANS 8:21

The doctrine of adoption tells us that the sum and substance of our promised inheritance is a share in the glory of Christ. We shall be made like our elder brother at every point, and sin and mortality—the double corruption of God's good work in the moral and spiritual spheres, respectively—will be things of the past. This, the blessing of resurrection day, will make actual for us all that was implicit in the relationship of adoption, for it will introduce us into the full experience of the heavenly life now enjoyed by our elder brother.

Paul dwells on the splendor of this event, assuring us that all creation, inarticulately yet really, is looking and longing "in eager expectation for the sons of God to be revealed" (Romans 8:19). Whatever else this passage may imply (and it was not written, let us remember, to satisfy the natural scientist's curiosity), it clearly underlines the surpassing grandeur of what awaits us in the good plan of God.

Journal: *Indulge in some sanctified creativity as you describe heaven when all creation, including yourself, is liberated from its "bondage to decay."*

Monday   *Hope*

We will be with the Lord forever. Therefore encourage each other with these words.

1 Thessalonians 4:17-18

*T*he doctrine of adoption tells us that the experience of heaven will be a family gathering, as the great host of the redeemed meet together in face-to-face fellowship with their Father God and Jesus their brother. This is the deepest and clearest idea of heaven that the Bible gives us.

"I see myself now at the end of my journey, my toilsome days are ended," said John Bunyan's Mr. Stand-fast as he stood halfway into Jordan's water. "The thought of what I am going to, and of the conduct that waits for me on the other side, doth lie as a glowing coal at my heart. . . . I have formerly lived by hearsay, and faith, but now I go where I shall live by sight, and shall be with him, in whose company I delight myself."

To see and know and love, and be loved by, the Father and the Son, in company with the rest of God's vast family, is the whole essence of the Christian hope.

Reflect: *In view of your current circumstances, how are you encouraged by the words above? Whom can you encourage with a similar hope?*

Tuesday

Quiet Work

God sent the Spirit of his Son into our hearts,
the Spirit who calls out, "Abba, Father."

GALATIANS 4:6

*O*ur adoption gives us the key to understanding the ministry of the Holy Spirit. We are all aware that the Spirit teaches the mind of God and glorifies the Son of God. We are aware that he is the agent of new birth, giving us an understanding so that we know God along with a new heart to obey him. We are aware that he indwells, sanctifies, and energizes Christians for their daily pilgrimage. We are aware, too, that assurance, joy, peace, and power are his special gifts. Yet some Christians feel they are missing something vital. In desperation they set themselves to seek a single transforming psychic event whereby what they feel to be their personal "unspirituality barrier" may be broken for good and all. But it is not as we strain after feelings and experiences but as we seek God himself, look to him as our Father, prizing his fellowship, and find in ourselves an increasing concern to know and please him that the reality of the Spirit's ministry becomes visible in our lives.

Reflect: *What are some of the Spirit's quiet works in your life? Thank him for these.*

Wednesday

The Spirit's Work

Dear friends, let us love one another,
for love comes from God.

1 JOHN 4:7

*T*he work of the Holy Spirit has three aspects.

In the first place, he makes and keeps us conscious—sometimes vividly conscious, but always conscious to some extent—that we are God's children by free grace through Jesus Christ. This is his work of giving faith, assurance, and joy.

In the second place, he moves us to look to God as to a father, showing toward him the respectful boldness and unlimited trust that is natural to children secure in an adored father's love. This is the work of making us cry, "Abba, Father."

In the third place, he impels us to act up to our position as royal children by manifesting the family likeness (conforming to Christ), furthering the family welfare (loving the brethren), and maintaining the family honor (seeking God's glory). This is his work of sanctification.

Journal: *Bring to mind a Christian whom you know and respect. How have you seen these and other evidences of the Spirit's work in this person's life? How has God's Spirit worked in your life through this person's example?*

Thursday

Gospel Holiness

Dear friends, now we are children of God, and what we will be has not yet been made known. But we know that when he appears, we shall be like him, for we shall see him as he is.

1 JOHN 3:2

*O*ur adoption shows us the meaning and motives of "gospel holiness." This phrase was Puritan shorthand for authentic Christian living, springing from love and gratitude to God.

First, gospel holiness is simply a consistent living out of our filial relationship with God. It is just a matter of the child of God being true to type—true to his Father, to his Savior, and to himself. It is the expressing of one's adoption in one's life.

Second, gospel holiness provides the motive for this authentically holy living. Christians know that God "predestinated us unto the adoption of children by Jesus Christ to himself" and that this involved his eternal intention that "we should be holy and without blame before him in love" (Ephesians 1:4-5 KJV). They know that they are moving toward a day when this destiny will be fully and finally realized. "When he appears, we shall be like him" (1 John 3:2).

Reflect: *How does your adoption into God's family provide both meaning and motive for "gospel holiness"?*

Friday

Chiseled Image

The Lord disciplines those he loves.

HEBREWS 12:6

The Christian up to his eyes in trouble can take comfort from the knowledge that in God's kindly plan it all has a positive purpose, namely to further his sanctification. In this world, royal children have to undergo extra training and discipline that other children escape, in order to fit them for their high destiny. It is the same with children of the King of kings. The clue to understanding all his dealings with them is to remember that throughout their lives he is training them for what awaits them and chiseling them into the image of Christ. Sometimes the chiseling process is painful and the discipline irksome, but then the Scripture reminds us: "The Lord disciplines those he loves." Only the person who has grasped this can make sense of Romans 8:28: "In all things God works for the good of those who love him."

Pray: *Up to your eyes in trouble? Pray for comfort stemming from your adoption as a child of God. Ask that any resulting chiseling will shape you willingly into the image of Christ.*

Saturday/Sunday

Forgiveness

> *[Jesus] said to them, "When you pray,*
> *say: . . . 'Forgive us our sins.'"*
>
> LUKE 11:2, 4

S ince justification means the pardon of all sin, past, present, and future, and complete acceptance for all eternity, why should we be concerned with whether we sin or not? Does it not show an imperfect grasp of justification when a Christian makes an issue of his daily sins and spends time mourning over them and seeking forgiveness? The Puritans had to face these "antinomian" ideas and sometimes made heavy weather answering them. The truth is that these questions must be answered in terms not of justification but of adoption.

What is the reply? It is this: that, while it is certainly true that justification frees one forever from the need to keep the law *as the means of earning life,* it is equally true that adoption lays on one the abiding obligation to keep the law *as the means of pleasing one's newfound Father.* Law keeping is the family likeness of God's children. If we sin, we confess our fault and ask our Father's forgiveness on the basis of the family relationship, as Jesus taught us to do.

Pray: *Spend a few moments in silence, asking God to reveal your sins, then confess them to him, asking his forgiveness and renewal.*

WEEK FORTY-TWO

Monday   *Assurance*

> *Those [God] predestined, he also called;*
> *those he called, he also justified;*
> *those he justified, he also glorified.*

ROMANS 8:30

*O*ur adoption gives us the clue we need to see our way through the problem of assurance. Here is a tangled skein if ever there was one! What is assurance? And whom does God assure—all believers, some, or none? When he assures, what does he assure of? And by what means is assurance given? The tangle is formidable, but the truth of adoption can help us unravel it.

If God in love has made Christians his children, and if he is perfect as a Father, then two things would seem to follow. First, the family relationship must be an abiding one, lasting forever. Perfect parents do not cast off their children. Christians may act the prodigal, but God will not cease to act the prodigal's father. Second, God will go out of his way to make his children feel his love for them and know their privilege and security as members of his family. Adopted children need assurance that they belong, and a perfect parent will not withhold it.

Reflect: *Throughout the coming day, draw your mind to God's love for you. Receive his assurance of your belonging to him.*

Tuesday   *No Separation*

> *I am convinced that neither death nor life,
> neither angels nor demons, neither the present
> nor the future, nor any powers, neither height
> nor depth, nor anything else in all creation,
> will be able to separate us from the love of
> God that is in Christ Jesus our Lord.*

ROMANS 8:38-39

*R*omans 8 is the New Testament passage on assurance. Paul tells us that those whom God "predestined to be conformed to the likeness of his Son, that he might be the firstborn among many brothers"—those, in other words, whom God eternally resolved to take as sons in his family, alongside his Only Begotten—"he called . . . justified . . . glorified" (Romans 8:29-30). "Glorified," we note, is in the past tense, though the event itself is still future. This shows that to Paul's mind the thing is as good as done already, being fixed in God's decree. Hence Paul's confidence in declaring, "I am convinced that neither death nor life . . . will be able to separate us from the love of God"—the electing, redeeming, paternal love of God—"that is in Christ Jesus our Lord."

Pray: *Meditate on each phrase of Romans 8:38-39, then pray your response to God, who holds you with this kind of love.*

Wednesday

Two Witnesses

Those who are led by the
Spirit of God are sons of God.

ROMANS 8:14

Paul tells us in Romans 8 that here and now "the Spirit himself testifies with our spirit that we are God's children" (verse 16). The statement is inclusive. Though Paul had never met the Romans, he felt able to take it for granted that if they were Christians, then they would know this inner witness of the Spirit to their happy status as sons and heirs of God.

In the New Testament, assurance is taken simply as a fact. We note that, in Romans 8:16, witness to our adoption is borne from two distinct sources: our spirit (that is, our conscious self) and God's Spirit, who bears witness *with* our spirit and so *to* our spirit. What is the nature of this dual witness? Robert Haldone writes that the witness of our spirit becomes a reality as "the Holy Spirit enables us to ascertain our sonship, from being conscious of, and discovering in ourselves, the true mark of renewed state."

Reflect: *What is the value of these two witnesses—God's Spirit and our spirit—joined together? How have you seen God's Spirit testifying to your own inner spirit? What impact does this interaction have on your praying, living, thinking?*

Thursday

Dual Witness

The Spirit himself testifies with our spirit that we are God's children.

ROMANS 8:16

*T*he truth about assurance comes out like this: our heavenly Father intends his children to know his love for them and know their own security in his family. He would not be the perfect Father if he did not want this and if he did not act to bring it about. His action takes the form of making the dual witness of his Spirit and our spirit part of the regular experience of his children. Thus he leads them to rejoice in his love. The dual witness is itself a gift—the crowning element in the complex gift of faith whereby believers gain "feeling knowledge" that their faith and adoption, the hope of heaven and the infinite sovereign love of God to them, are all "really real." Of this dimension of faith's experience, it's likely to be more easily felt than told. Yet all Christians ordinarily enjoy it to some extent, for it is in truth part of their birthright.

Journal: *Write an attempt to tell the story about the impact of this dual witness in your own experience of knowing God.*

Friday   *Assurance Tested*

*Dear children, let us not love with words
or tongue but with actions and in truth.*

1 JOHN 3:18

Assurance is the direct work of the Spirit in the regenerate heart, coming in to supplement the God-prompted witness of our own spirit. While this dual witness can be temporarily clouded through divine withdrawal and satanic assault, every wholehearted Christian who is not grieving and quenching the Spirit by unfaithfulness ordinarily enjoys both aspects of the witness. Being prone to self-deception, we do well to test our assurance by applying the doctrinal and ethical concerns that 1 John provides for this purpose (see 1 John 2:3, 29; 3:6-10, 14, 18-21; 4:7-8, 15-16; 5:1-4, 18). By this means the inferential element in our assurance will be strengthened and the vividness of assurance may vastly increase. The source of assurance, however, is not simply our inferences but the work of the Spirit, apart from as well as through our inferences, convincing us that we are God's children and that the saving love and promises of God apply directly to us.

Journal: *As a self-test, read each of the passages from 1 John listed above. Journal ways in which each builds (or challenges) your assurance that you are adopted into God's family.*

Saturday/Sunday   *Self-Check*

If anyone is in Christ, he is a new creation;
the old has gone, the new has come!
All this is from God, who reconciled us
to himself through Christ.

2 CORINTHIANS 5:17-18

*T*he immediate message of adoption to our hearts is surely this: Do I, as a Christian, understand myself? Do I know my own real identity? my own real destiny? *I am a child of God. God is my Father; heaven is my home; every day is one day nearer. My Savior is my brother; every Christian is my brother too.* Say it over and over to yourself first thing in the morning, last thing at night, as you wait in traffic, any time when your mind is free, and ask that you may be enabled to live as one who knows it all to be utterly and completely true. For this is the Christian's secret (of a happy life?—yes, certainly, but we have something both higher and profounder to say). This is the Christian's secret of a *Christian* life, of a *God-honoring* life, and these are the aspects of the situation that really matter. May this secret become fully yours and fully mine.

Reflect: *Meditate on the italicized statement of purpose above. Put it in a prominent place for frequent review.*

Monday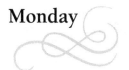

Adoption Ideals

*You, O LORD, are our Father, our
Redeemer from of old is your name.*

ISAIAH 63:16

To help us realize more adequately who and what, as children of God, we are and are called to be, here are some questions by which we do well to examine ourselves again and again. Do I understand my adoption? Do I value it? Do I daily remind myself of my privilege as a child of God? Have I sought full assurance of my adoption? Do I daily dwell on the love of God to me? Do I treat God as my Father in heaven, loving, honoring, and obeying him, seeking and welcoming his fellowship, and trying in everything to please him as a human parent would want their child to do? Do I think of Jesus Christ, my Savior and my Lord, as my brother too, bearing to me not only a divine authority but also a divine-human sympathy? Do I think daily how close he is to me, how completely he understands me and how much, as my Kinsman-redeemer, he cares for me?

Reflect: *From the paragraph above, select one question per day for today and each of the next seven days. Use it as a question of examination and as a goal for living with joy under the umbrella of God's adoption.*

Tuesday

Self-Inquiry

*We know that we have passed from death
to life, because we love our brothers.*

1 John 3:14

*A*s we conclude our devotionals on adoption into God's family, here are further questions for self-inquiry. Am I sensitive to the evil things to which my Father is sensitive? Do I make a point of avoiding them, lest I grieve him? Do I look forward daily to that great family occasion when the children of God will finally gather in heaven before the throne of God, their Father, and of the Lamb, their brother and their Lord? Have I felt the thrill of this hope? Do I love my Christian brothers and sisters with whom I live day by day in a way that I shall not be ashamed of when in heaven I think back over it? Am I proud of my Father and of his family, to which by his grace I belong? Does the family likeness appear in me? If not, why not?

God humble us. God instruct us. God make us his own true children.

Pray: *Select one question above (saving the others for a later time) and use it as a basis for prayer, expressing any needed confession and any joy of thanksgiving.*

Wednesday   *God's Guidance*

> *Since you are my rock and my fortress, for*
> *the sake of your name lead and guide me.*

*T*o many Christians, guidance is a chronic problem. Why? Not because they doubt that divine guidance is a fact but because they are sure that it is. They know that God can guide, and has promised to guide, every Christian believer. Books and friends and public speakers tell them how guidance has worked in the lives of others. Their fear, therefore, is not that no guidance should be available for them but that they may miss the guidance that God provides through some fault of their own. With William Williams they sing,

> Guide me, O thou great Jehovah, pilgrim through this
>   barren land;
> I am weak, but Thou art mighty, hold me with Thy
>   powerful hand:
> Bread of heaven feed me now and evermore.

And they have no doubt that God is able both to lead and to feed, as they ask. But they remain anxious because they are not certain of their own receptiveness to the guidance God offers.

Journal: *Write a list of questions that come to your mind regarding God's guidance.*

Thursday   *God's Plan*

> *[God's] intent was that now, through the church, the manifold wisdom of God should be made known, . . . according to his eternal purpose which he accomplished in Christ Jesus our Lord.*

> EPHESIANS 3:10-11

*B*elief that divine guidance is real rests on two foundational facts: first, the reality of God's plan for us; second, the ability of God to communicate with us. On both of these facts the Bible has much to say.

Has God a plan for individuals? Indeed he has. He has formed an "eternal purpose" (literally, a "plan for the ages"). He had a plan for the redemption of his people from Egyptian bondage when he guided them through the sea and the desert by means of a pillar of cloud by day and a pillar of fire by night. He had a plan for Jesus (Luke 22:22)—Jesus' whole business on earth was to do his Father's will (John 4:34). God had a plan for Paul (see Acts 21:14)—in five of his letters Paul announces himself as an apostle "by the will of God." God has a plan for each of his children.

Journal: *"God has a plan for each of his children." Journal your response to this statement.*

Friday

Guided with Purpose

I will instruct you and teach you
in the way you should go.

PSALM 32:8

$\mathcal{C}$an God communicate his plan to us? Indeed he can. As man is a communicative animal, so his Maker is a communicative God. He made known his will to and through the Old Testament prophets. He guided Jesus and Paul. Acts records several instances of detailed guidance (Philip being sent to the desert to meet the Ethiopian eunuch, Acts 8:26, 29; Peter being told to accept the invitation of Cornelius, Acts 10:19-29; the church at Antioch being charged to send Paul and Barnabas as missionaries, Acts 13:2; Paul and Silas being called into Europe, Acts 16:6-10; Paul being instructed to press on with his Corinthian ministry, Acts 18:9-10). And though guidance by dreams, visions, and direct verbal messages must be judged exceptional and not normal, even for the apostles and their contemporaries, these events do at least show that God has no difficulty in making his will known to his servants.

Reflect: *Read the biblical account of one of the examples above. What does it reveal of God's purpose as he guided this particular follower?*

Saturday/Sunday

Confidence

He guides me in paths of
righteousness for his name's sake.

PSALM 23:3

*B*iblical truth confirms our confidence that God will guide.

First, Christians are God's children. If human parents have a responsibility to give their children guidance in matters where ignorance and incapacity would spell danger, we should not doubt that in the family of God the same applies.

Second, Scripture is God's Word, "profitable for teaching, for reproof, for correction, and for training in righteousness, that the man of God may be complete" (2 Timothy 3:16-17 RSV).

Third, Christians have an indwelling Instructor, the Holy Spirit. It is notable that in the decree of the Jerusalem Council guidance is specifically ascribed to the Spirit. "It has seemed good to the Holy Spirit and to us . . ." (Acts 15:28).

Fourth, God seeks his glory in our lives, and he is glorified in us only when we obey his will. It follows that, as a means to his own end, he must be ready to teach us his way so that we may walk in it.

It is impossible to doubt that guidance is a reality intended for, and promised to, every child of God.

Pray: *Thank God for the four aspects of his guidance illustrated above.*

Monday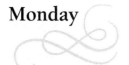

Guidance Gone Wrong

> *In all thy ways acknowledge him,*
> *and he shall direct thy paths.*

PROVERBS 3:6 KJV

*E*arnest Christians seeking guidance often go wrong. Why is this? Often the reason is that their notion of the nature and method of divine guidance is distorted. They look for a misleading hope; they overlook the guidance that is ready at hand and lay themselves open to all sorts of delusions. Their basic mistake is to think of guidance as essentially inward prompting by the Holy Spirit, apart from the written Word. This idea is a seedbed in which all forms of fanaticism and folly can grow.

How do thoughtful Christians come to make this mistake? What seems to happen is this. They hear the word *guidance* and think at once of a particular class of "guidance problems." This is the class of problems concerned with "vocational choices"—choices, that is, among competing options, all of which in themselves appear lawful and good. Should I marry this person or not? Should we aim at having a child? Should I join this church or that one? Which job should I take?

Reflect: *How are the vocational questions above similar to or different from examples of God's guidance in Scripture?*

Tuesday

Vocational Choices

Show me your ways, O Lord,
teach me your paths.

Psalm 25:4

*W*e think a lot about "vocational choices," and it is right that we should. But what is not right is to jump to the conclusion that all guidance problems are of this one type.

Two features about divine guidance in the case of "vocational choices" are distinctive. First, these problems cannot be resolved by a direct application of biblical teaching. No biblical text, for instance, told the present writer to propose to the lady who is now his wife, to seek ordination, to start his ministry in England, or to buy his large old car. Second, just because Scripture cannot decide one choice directly, the factor of God-given prompting and inclination that finds one's mind settled in peace as one contemplates one choice over the other becomes decisive. But it is a mistake to think that all of life should be treated as a field in which this kind of guidance should be sought.

Reflect: *How might "God's ways" of Psalm 25 guide some vocational choices but not others?*

Wednesday

Lunacy?

I . . . want women to dress modestly,
with decency and propriety.

1 TIMOTHY 2:9

$\mathcal{T}$he idea of a life in which the inward voice of the Spirit decides and directs everything sounds most attractive, for it seems to exalt the Spirit's ministry and to promise the closest intimacy with God. But in practice this quest for superspirituality leads only to frantic bewilderment or lunacy.

Hannah Whitall Smith, that commonsensical Quaker lady, saw much of this and wrote of it instructively in her "fanaticism papers." There she tells of the woman who each morning, having consecrated the day to the Lord as soon as she woke, "would then ask him whether she was to get up or not" and would not stir till "the voice" told her to dress. "As she put on each article she asked the Lord whether she was to put it on, and very often the Lord would tell her to put on the right shoe and leave off the other; sometimes she was to put on both stockings and no shoes; and sometimes both shoes and no stocking; it was the same with all the articles of dress."

We need to find a balanced perspective on guidance that will allow us to seek and find God on a daily basis while still using the mind he has given us.

Reflect: *What precautions would you recommend to prevent "guidance" toward lunacy?*

Thursday

Rational Guidance

*He guides me in paths of
righteousness for his name's sake.*

PSALM 23:3

Our rational Creator guides his rational creatures by rational understanding and application of his written Word. This mode of guidance is fundamental, both because it limits the area within which "vocational" guidance is needed and given and also because only those who have attuned themselves to it, so that their basic attitudes are right, are likely to be able to recognize "vocational" guidance when it comes. Only within the limits of *this* guidance does God prompt us inwardly in matters of "vocational" decision. So never expect to be guided to marry an unbeliever, or elope with a married person, as long as 1 Corinthians 7:39 and the seventh commandment stand! The present writer has known divine guidance to be claimed for both courses of action. Inward inclinations were undoubtedly present, but they were quite certainly not from the Spirit of God, for they went against the Word.

The Spirit leads within the limits that the Word sets, not beyond them. "He guides me in *paths of righteousness*"—but not anywhere else.

Reflect: *How might righteousness, as Scripture teaches it, guide one of your current decisions?*

Friday

Ethical Highway

Turn from evil and do good.

PSALM 34:14

$\mathcal{T}$he basic form of divine guidance is the presentation to us of positive ideals as guidelines for all our living. "Be the kind of person that Jesus was." "Seek this virtue, and this one, and this, and practice them up to the limit." "Know your responsibilities—husbands to your wives, wives to your husbands, parents to your children, all of you to all your fellow Christians and all your fellow human beings. Know them, and seek strength constantly to discharge them." This is how God guides us through the Bible, as any student of the Psalms, the Proverbs, the Prophets, the Sermon on the Mount, and the ethical parts of the Epistles will soon discover.

"Turn from evil and do good" (Psalm 34:14; 37:27)—this is the highway along which the Bible is concerned to lead us, and all its admonitions are concerned to keep us on it.

Pray: *Thank God for the system of ethics that Scripture gives for the people of God—and for the character he builds in those who walk that ethical highway.*

Saturday/Sunday   *Thinking Ahead*

O that they were wise, . . . that they
would consider their latter end!

*T*he work of God in vocational guidance is to incline first our judgment and then our whole being to the course that, of all the competing alternatives, he has marked out as best suited for us and for his glory and the good of others through us. But the Spirit can be quenched, so it is worth listing some of the main pitfalls to receiving that guidance.

First, unwillingness to think. It is false piety, super-supernaturalism of an unhealthy and pernicious sort, that demands inward impressions that have no rational base and declines to heed the constant biblical summons to "consider." God made us thinking beings, and he guides our minds as in his presence we think things out—not otherwise.

Second, unwillingness to think ahead and weigh the long-term consequences of alternative courses of action blocks God's guidance. "Think ahead" is part of the divine rule of life no less than the human rule of the road. Often we can see what is wise and right (and what is foolish and wrong) only as we dwell on its long-term issues.

Reflect: *Consider potential long-term results of a current decision. Ask God to guide your thinking.*

WEEK FORTY-FIVE

Monday   *Advice*

> *The way of a fool seems right to him,*
> *but a wise man listens to advice.*

PROVERBS 12:15

There are several potential barriers to receiving God's guidance in "vocational choices."

Unwillingness to take advice is one such barrier. It is a sign of conceit and immaturity to dispense with taking advice in major decisions. There are always people who know the Bible, human nature, and our own gifts and limitations better than we do, and even if we cannot finally accept their advice, nothing but good will come to us from carefully weighing what they say.

Likewise, an unwillingness to suspect oneself is a barrier. We need to ask ourselves why we "feel" a particular course to be right and to make ourselves give reasons, and we will be wise to lay the case before someone else whose judgment we trust, to give a verdict on our reasons. We need also to keep praying, "Search me, O God, and know my heart: try me, and know my thoughts: and see if there be any wicked way in me, and lead me in the way everlasting" (Psalm 139:23-24 KJV). We can never distrust ourselves too much.

Journal: *Recall in writing a time when someone's advice pointed you in the right direction. If appropriate, send that person a note of thanks.*

Tuesday

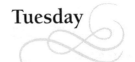

Be Wary

Test everything. Hold on to the good.

1 THESSALONIANS 5:21

*A*s in the preceding couple of devotionals, we continue looking at pitfalls in the way of receiving God's guidance.

Unwillingness to discount personal magnetism can be a pitfall. Well-meaning but deluded people with a flair for self-dramatization can gain an alarming domination over the minds and consciences of others. But this is not the way to be led by God. Outstanding people are not necessarily wrong, but they are not necessarily right, either! They and their views must be respected but should not be idolized. "Test everything. Hold on to the good" (1 Thessalonians 5:21).

Unwillingness to wait can be another pitfall to guidance. "Wait on the Lord" is a constant refrain in the Psalms, and it is a necessary word, for God often keeps us waiting. He is not in such a hurry as we are, and it is not his way to give more light on the future than we need for action in the present or to guide us more than one step at a time. When in doubt, do nothing, but continue to wait on God. When action is needed, light will come.

Reflect: *What do you know about yourself that would help (or hinder) avoiding the two pitfalls described above to receiving God's guidance?*

Wednesday

Trouble

> *I desire to speak to the Almighty*
> *and to argue my case with God.*

JOB 13:3

Sometimes in the Christian life we seek guidance from God and believe it has been given. We then set off along the road that God seemed to indicate. And now, as a direct result, we run into a crop of new problems that otherwise would not have arisen—isolation, criticism, abandonment by friends, practical frustrations of all sorts. At once we grow anxious. However, it does not follow that right guidance will be vindicated as such by a trouble-free course thereafter. What we do know is that we will walk our course with God, which is how we are meant to live.

Reflect: *In view of what you know of God through Scripture and your own experience, how would you advise a person experiencing what is described above?*

Thursday

Taking the Wrong Ship

The word of the LORD came to Jonah son of Amittai: "Go to the great city of Nineveh and preach against it, because its wickedness has come up before me." But Jonah ran away from the LORD and headed for Tarshish.

JONAH 1:1-3

In times when following what we understand to be God's guidance is rough, we may recall the prophet Jonah. This prophet, when told to go east and preach at Nineveh, instead took a ship going north to Tarshish, "away from the LORD" (Jonah 1:3).

Is our own present experience of the rough side of life (we ask ourselves) a sign from God that we are ourselves like Jonah, off track, following the path of self-will rather than the way of God? It may be so, and the wise person will take occasion from his new troubles to check his original guidance carefully. Trouble should always be treated as a call to consider one's ways.

Pray: *Ask the Lord about any direction you are taking that seems uncertain to you. Ask him to clarify his will for you in this area.*

Friday   *Darkness*

A righteous man may have many troubles,
but the LORD delivers him from them all.

PSALM 34:19

*T*rouble is not necessarily a sign of being off track in one's life decisions.

Look at the example of Paul. The apostle crossed to Greece, concluding from his dream of the man of Macedonia "that God had called us to preach the gospel to them" (Acts 16:10). Before long he was in jail at Philippi.

Look at the life of the Lord Jesus himself. No human life has ever been so completely guided by God, and no human being has ever qualified so comprehensively for the description "a man of sorrows." Divine guidance set Jesus at a distance from his family and fellow townsmen, brought him into conflict with all the nation's leaders, religious and civil, and led finally to betrayal, arrest, and the cross. What more can Christians expect while they abide in the will of God? "A student is not above his teacher, nor a servant above his master" (Matthew 10:24).

Sooner or later, God's guidance, which brings us out of darkness into light, will also bring us out of light into darkness. It is part of the way of the cross.

Journal: *When have you experienced the dark way of the cross? What have you learned about God from that time?*

Saturday/Sunday   *Locust Years*

> *I will repay you for the years the locusts*
> *have eaten. . . . You will have plenty to eat,*
> *until you are full, and you will praise*
> *the name of the Lord your God.*

> JOEL 2:25-26

If I found I had driven into a bog, I would know I had missed the road. But this knowledge would not be of much comfort if I then had to stand helpless while watching the car sink and vanish. The damage would be done, and that would be that.

Is it the same when a Christian wakes up to the fact that he has missed God's guidance and taken the wrong way? Is the damage irrevocable? Must he now be put off course for life? Thank God, no.

Our God is a God who not merely restores but also takes up our mistakes and follies into his plan for us and brings good out of them. This is part of the wonder of his gracious sovereignty. "I will repay you for the years the locusts have eaten." God makes not only the wrath of man to turn to his praise but the misadventures of Christians too.

Journal: *Journal an account of God's kindness to you or someone you know in the wake of "locust years."*

Monday   *Lord Protector*

> *This is what the Sovereign Lord*
> *says: I myself will search for my*
> *sheep and look after them.*

> **Ezekiel 34:11**

*G*uidance, like all God's acts of blessing under the covenant of grace, is a sovereign act. Not merely does God will to guide us in the sense of showing us his way, that we may tread in it; he wills also to guide us in the more fundamental sense of ensuring that, whatever happens, whatever mistakes we may make, we will come safely home. Slipping and straying there will be, no doubt, but the everlasting arms are beneath us. We will be caught, rescued, restored. This is God's promise; this is how good he is.

God will not let us ruin our souls. Our concern, therefore, should be more for his glory than for our security, for that is already taken care of. And our self-distrust, while keeping us humble, must not cloud the joy with which we lean on "the Lord Protector"—our faithful covenant God.

Pray: *In prayer, offer your response to our "Lord Protector," who "will not let us ruin our souls."*

Tuesday

Trouble Free?

*We must go through many hardships
to enter the kingdom of God.*

ACTS 14:22

*W*hen we talk about the gospel, we must tell the whole truth. We may be tempted to make false promises about the difference that becoming a Christian will make. We may not stop at declaring that salvation will bring us forgiveness of sins, peace of conscience, and fellowship with God as our Father. We may go on to claim it also means that, through the power of the indwelling Spirit, we will be able to overcome the sins that previously mastered us. We may claim that the light and leading that God will give us will enable us to find a way through problems of guidance, self-fulfillment, personal relationships, heart's desire, and suchlike that had hitherto defeated us completely.

This is to suggest that the world, the flesh, and the devil will give us no serious trouble once we are Christians. Nor will our circumstances and personal relationships ever be a problem to us. Nor will we ever be a problem to ourselves. Such suggestions are mischievous, however, because they are false. To picture the normal Christian life as trouble free is bound to lead sooner or later to bitter disillusionment.

Reflect: *What problems can you foresee for a new Christian invited into the faith with the suggestion that life will be much easier and happier in this new spiritual state?*

Wednesday

Relapse

What I do is not the good I want to do;
no, the evil I do not want to do—
this I keep on doing.

ROMANS 7:19

A preacher wants to win his hearers to Christ, so he glamorizes the Christian life, making it sound as happy and carefree as he can, in order to allure unbelievers. On this basis, they are converted, experience the new birth, and advance into their new life joyfully certain that they have left all the old headaches and heartaches behind them.

And then they find that it is not like that at all. Long-standing problems of personal relationships, of nagging temptations are still there—sometimes, indeed, intensified. Dissatisfaction recurs over wife or husband or parents or in-laws or children or colleagues or neighbors. As the first great waves of joy rolled over them during the opening weeks of their Christian experience, they had really felt that all problems had solved themselves, but now they see that it was not so. What are they to think now?

Journal: *If this new convert were your friend, what would you advise?*

Thursday

Conditioning Exercises

*God is faithful. . . . When you are
tempted, he will . . . provide a way out
so that you can stand up under it.*

1 CORINTHIANS 10:13

*G*od is gentle with young Christians, just as mothers are with babies. Often the start of their Christian career is marked by great emotional joy, striking providence, remarkable answers to prayer, and immediate fruitfulness to their first acts of witness. Thus God encourages them.

But as they grow stronger and are able to bear more, he exercises them in a tougher school. He exposes them to as much testing as they are able to bear. Thus he builds our character, strengthens our faith, and prepares us to help others. Thus he crystallizes our sense of values. Thus he glorifies himself in our lives, making his strength perfect in our weakness.

There is nothing unnatural, therefore, in an increase of temptations, conflicts, and pressures as the Christian goes on with God. Indeed, something would be wrong if it did not happen.

Journal: *When has a difficult experience in your own life had some of the strengthening effects described here?*

Friday

Restoration

> *Wash away all my iniquity*
> *and cleanse me from my sin. For I*
> *know my transgressions, and my*
> *sin is always before me.*

PSALM 51:2-3

*I*f Christians grow careless toward God and slip back into ways of deliberate sin, their inward joy and rest of heart grow less, and discontent of spirit comes to mark them more and more. Those who through union with Christ are "dead to sin" (Romans 6:11)—done with it, that is, as the ruling principle of their lives—cannot find in sinning even that limited pleasure that it gave them before they were reborn. Nor can they indulge in wrong ways without imperiling their enjoyment of God's favor—God will see to that!

Unregenerate apostates are often cheerful souls, but backsliding Christians are always miserable. The remedy, therefore, is for this lapsed Christian to find, confess, and forsake his defection. It is to reconsecrate himself to Christ. It is to learn the habit, when problems and temptations come, of handing them over to Christ to deal with for him.

Reflect: *What do you find spiritually good and healthy about the restoration process described above? What do you find worrisome—if it were to happen over and over?*

Saturday/Sunday

Intentional Trial

> *These [trials] have come so that*
> *your faith—of greater worth than gold,*
> *which perishes even though refined*
> *by fire—may be proved genuine.*

*S*ooner or later, the truth will be that God exercises his child—his consecrated child—in the ways of adult godliness by exposing him to strong attacks from the world, the flesh, and the devil so that his powers of resistance might grow greater and his character as a man of God become stronger. And if this is what is happening to the perplexed Christian, then seeking a return of new-believer joy will be disastrous. For what would it do? This practice sentences devoted Christians to a treadmill life of hunting each day for nonexistent failures in consecration, in the belief that if only they could find some such failures to confess and forsake, they could recover an experience of spiritual infancy that God means them to now leave behind. God has taken from them the carefree glow of spiritual babyhood, with its huge chuckles and contented passivity, precisely in order that he may lead them into an experience that is more adult and mature.

Pray: *Ask God for courage to grow in circumstances that remove joy and stifle feelings of faith.*

Monday   *Will and Work*

> *By the grace of God I am what I am,*
> *and his grace to me was not without effect.*
> *No, I worked harder than all of them—yet not I,*
> *but the grace of God that was with me.*

1 CORINTHIANS 15:10

*W*hat is grace? In the New Testament, grace means God's love in action toward people who merited the opposite of love. Grace means God moving heaven and earth to save sinners who could not lift a finger to save themselves.

The New Testament knows both a *will* of grace and a *work* of grace. The former is God's eternal plan to save; the latter is God's "good work in you" (Philippians 1:6), whereby he calls you into living fellowship with Christ (1 Corinthians 1:9). Look, for instance, at 1 Corinthians 15:10 above. The word "grace" clearly denotes God's loving work in Paul, whereby he made him first a Christian and then a minister. And so we each can offer praise that "by the grace of God I am what I am."

Journal: *In what ways has God worked both the will and the work of grace in your own life?*

Tuesday

Rock and Refuge

The LORD is my rock, my fortress and my deliverer; my God is my rock in whom I take refuge.

PSALM 18:2

What is the purpose of grace? Primarily, to restore our relationship with God. Grace is God drawing us sinners closer and closer to himself.

How does God in grace prosecute this purpose? Not by shielding us from assault by the world, nor by protecting us from burdensome and frustrating circumstances, nor yet by shielding us from troubles created by our own temperament. Rather, by exposing us to all these things, so as to overwhelm us with a sense of our own inadequacy and to drive us to cling to him more closely.

Why does God fill our lives with troubles and perplexities of one sort and another? To ensure that we will learn to hold them fast. This is why the Bible spends so much of its time reiterating that God is a strong rock, a firm defense, and a sure refuge and help for the weak.

Journal: *Create a prayer describing ways that God is and has been your rock and your refuge.*

Wednesday

Wait

> *They that wait upon the Lord shall*
> *renew their strength; they shall mount up*
> *with wings as eagles; they shall run, and not be*
> *weary; and they shall walk, and not faint.*

Isaiah 40:31 KJV

When we walk along a clear road feeling fine and someone takes our arm to help us, as likely as not we will impatiently shake him off. But when we are caught in rough country in the dark, with a storm getting up and our strength spent, and someone takes our arm to help us, we will thankfully lean on him.

God wants us to feel that our way through life is rough and perplexing so that we may learn thankfully to lean on him. Therefore he takes steps to drive us out of self-confidence and into trust in himself—in the classical scriptural phrase for the secret of the godly life, to "wait on the Lord."

Pray: *Use the words of Isaiah 40:31 as an outline for prayer. Begin each section of your prayer with a line from the text.*

Thursday

Mistakes

The LORD longs to be gracious to you;
he rises to show you compassion.

ISAIAH 30:18

It is striking to see how much of the Bible deals with godly people making mistakes and God chastening them for it. Abraham, promised a son but made to wait for him, loses patience and begets Ishmael. David makes a run of mistakes: seducing Bathsheba and getting Uriah killed, neglecting his family, numbering the people for prestige. Jonah makes the mistake of running away from God's call—and finds himself inside a great fish. The point is that the human mistake and the immediate divine displeasure were in no case the end of the story. God can bring good out of the extremes of our own folly. God can restore the years that the locusts have eaten. It is said that those who never make mistakes never make anything. Through their mistakes, God taught these men to know his grace and to cleave to him in a way that would never have happened otherwise.

Is your trouble a sense of failure? The knowledge of having made some ghastly mistake? Go back to God. His restoring grace waits for you.

Journal: *In writing, reflect on one of your mistakes. Invite God's grace and restoration.*

Friday

Rescue

*What a wretched man I am! Who will
rescue me from this body of death?*

ROMANS 7:24

*I*n the hymn that he titled "Prayer Answered by Crosses," John
Newton wrote the following:

> I asked the Lord, that I might grow in faith, and love, and
> every grace;
> Might more of His salvation know and seek more earnestly
> His face.
>
> I hoped that in some favoured hour at once He'd answer my
> request,
> And by His love's constraining power subdue my sins, and
> give me rest.
>
> Instead of this, He made me feel the hidden evils of my heart;
> And let the angry powers of hell assault my soul in every part.
>
> "Lord, why is this?" I trembling cried, "Wilt thou pursue Thy
> worm to death?"
> "'Tis in this way," the Lord replied, "I answer prayer for grace
> and faith.
>
> "These inward trials I employ from self and pride to set thee free;
> And break thy schemes of earthly joy, that thou may'st seek
> thy all in me."

Pray: *Talk to God about some of your own "inward trials." Seek
grace and faith from him.*

Saturday/Sunday

Getting the Message

Paul, a servant of Christ Jesus,
called to be an apostle and set apart
for the gospel of God. . . . To all in
Rome who are loved by God
and called to be saints . . .

ROMANS 1:1, 7

*P*aul's letter to Rome is the high peak of Scripture, however you look at it. Luther called it "the clearest gospel of all." "If a man understands it," wrote John Calvin, "he has a sure road opened to him to the understanding of the whole Scripture." William Tyndale, in his preface to Romans, linked both thoughts, calling Romans "the principal and most excellent part of the New Testament . . . that is to say glad tidings and what we call gospel, and also a light and a way in unto the whole Scripture."

All roads in the Bible lead to Romans, and all views afforded by the Bible are seen most clearly from Romans. When the message of Romans gets into a person's heart, there is no telling what may happen.

Reflect: *Page through the book of Romans, stopping to read arresting ideas that catch your eye in each chapter.*

Monday   *The Whole Gospel*

*I urge you, brothers, in view of
God's mercy, to offer your bodies as living
sacrifices, holy and pleasing to God—
this is your spiritual act of worship.*

ROMANS 12:1

What do you look for in the Bible? Is it doctrine—truth about God, taught by God? If so, you will find that Romans gives you all the main themes integrated together: God, man, sin, law, judgment, faith, works, grace, creation, redemption, justification, sanctification, the plan of salvation, election, reprobation, the person and work of Christ, the work of the Spirit, the Christian hope, the nature of the church, the place of Jew and Gentile in God's purpose, the philosophy of the church and world history, the meaning and message of the Old Testament, the significance of baptism, the principles of personal piety and ethics, the duties of Christian citizenship—et cetera!

But the wise person also reads the Bible as a book of life. What has Romans to offer here? The answer is this: the fullest cross-section of the life of sin and life of grace and the deepest analysis of the way of faith that the Bible gives anywhere.

Pray: *Ask for a discerning mind and a will bent toward following Christ as you follow the final sequence of devotionals in this book, based largely on Romans.*

Tuesday

Book of the Church

*In Christ we who are many
form one body, and each member
belongs to all the others.*

ROMANS 12:5

*O*ne way of reading the Bible is as a book of the church, where the God-given faith and self-understanding of the believing fellowship are voiced. From this standpoint, Romans, just because it is the classic statement of the gospel by which the church lives, is also the classic account of the church's identity.

What is the church? It is the true seed of faithful Abraham, Jew and non-Jew together, chosen by God, justified through faith and freed from sin for a new life of personal righteousness and mutual ministry. It is the family of a loving heavenly Father, living in hope of inheriting his entire fortune. It is the community of the resurrection, in which the powers of Christ's historic death and present heavenly life are already at work. And nowhere is this presented so fully as in Romans.

Reflect: *In what ways does your own church reflect the description of the church given above?*

Wednesday   *Personal Letter*

*Those who live according to the sinful nature
have their minds set on what that nature desires; but those who live in accordance with
the Spirit have their minds set on what the
Spirit desires.*

ROMANS 8:5

$\mathcal{T}$he wise person reads the Bible as God's personal letter to each
of his spiritual children and therefore to him as much as to
anyone. Read Romans this way and you will find that it has
unique power to search out and deal with things that are so
much part of you that ordinarily you do not give them a thought—
your sinful habits and attitudes; your instinct for hypocrisy; your
natural self-righteousness and self-reliance; your constant unbelief; your moral frivolity and shallowness in repentance; your
halfheartedness, worldliness, fearfulness, and despondency; your
spiritual conceit and insensitivity. And you will also find that this
shattering letter has unique power to evoke the joy, assurance,
boldness, liberty, and ardor of spirit that God both requires of
and gives to those who love him. It was said of Jonathan Edwards
that his doctrine was all application and his application was all
doctrine. Romans is supremely like that.

Journal: *What would you like to see God accomplish in you
through your focus on Romans?*

Thursday  *The Peak*

> *In the gospel a righteousness from*
> *God is revealed, . . . just as it is written:*
> *"The righteous will live by faith."*
>
> ROMANS 1:17

*S*omeone who touched down on the top of Everest in a helicopter (could such a thing be) would not at that moment feel anything like what Edmund Hillary and Tenzing Norgay felt when they stood on the same spot *after climbing the mountain.* Similarly, the impact of Romans on you will depend on what has gone before. The more you have dug into the rest of the Bible, the more you are exercised with the intellectual and moral problems of being a Christian. And the more you have felt the burden of weakness and the strain of faithfulness in your Christian life, the more you will find Romans saying to you. John Chrysostom had it read aloud to him once a week; you and I could do a lot worse than that.

Reflect: *Follow the wisdom of John Chrysostom and (lacking a servant reader) read aloud the book of Romans as if it were a personal letter to you and to your church.*

Friday

Romans Ready

Since we have now been justified by his blood, how much more shall we be saved from God's wrath through him!

ROMANS 5:9

As Romans is the high peak of the Bible, so chapter 8 is the high peak of Romans. You will not penetrate the secret of Romans 8 by studying the chapter on its own. The way into Romans 8 is through Romans 1–7.

First you must come to know yourself as a lost and helpless sinner (chapters 1–3). Then, with Abraham, you must trust the divine promise that seems too good to be true in your case, namely the promise of acceptance because Jesus, your covenant head, died and rose (chapters 4–5). Next, as a new creature in Christ, you must commit yourself to total holiness and then find in yourself that the flesh is at war with the spirit, so that you live in contradiction, never fully achieving the good you purposed nor avoiding all the evil you renounced (chapters 6–7). Only if, on top of this, "losses and crosses" are upon you, will Romans 8 yield up its full riches and make its great power known to you.

Journal: *What do you see of yourself in the description of those prepared to "penetrate the secret of Romans 8"?*

Saturday/Sunday *Wretchedness*

> *I find this law at work: When I want to*
> *do good, evil is right there with me.*

ROMANS 7:21

*W*hy did Paul write Romans 8? The short answer—not as silly as it sounds—is this: because he had just written Romans 7! In Romans 7:7 Paul had raised the question, is the law sin? The answer he had to give was this: no, but the law is a source of sinning. The law actually foments what it forbids and so stirs up the impulse to disobey, such that the more a person sets himself to keep the law, the more he finds himself transgressing it.

To show this in the quickest and most vivid way, Paul had described his own experience of it. As he described this, his reaction had welled up spontaneously: "What a wretched man I am! Who will rescue me from this body of death?" (Romans 7:24). The question was rhetorical, for he knew that total deliverance from sin came through Christ. But for the present, he had to bear the bitter experience of being unable to attain the perfection he sought, because the law that required it was powerless to induce it.

Journal: *What are some of your own frustrations with yourself and God's law?*

Monday 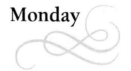 *Law and Gospel*

> *I myself in my mind am a*
> *slave to God's law, but in the sinful*
> *nature a slave to the law of sin.*

ROMANS 7:25

$\mathcal{B}$y the end of Romans 7, Paul has shown that the law speaks not of privilege and achievement but only of failure and guilt. For sensitive Christians who know how God hates sin, to be diagnosed by the law is a depressing experience. Writing these verses had clouded Paul's own joy, and as a good pastor, always thinking of the effect of his words, he knew that reading them would spread the gloom. But he does not think it right to leave the Roman Christians contemplating the sad side of their experience and feeling as if they were back under the law. Instead, he reminds them at once that what is decisive is not what the law says about them but what the gospel says. So, by a logic both evangelical and pastoral, Paul picks up the theme of Christian assurance and develops it as forcibly as he can, from "no condemnation" at the start to "no separation" at the close.

Reflect: *Read without interruption from Romans 7:7–8:39. What do you appreciate about this connection between law and gospel?*

Tuesday   *Think*

What . . . shall we say in response to this?

ROMANS 8:31

*I*n Romans 8:31 Paul asks his readers to speak. But he first calls on them to think. He knows two factors common to all real Christians. The first is commitment to all-around righteousness. The second is exposure to all-around pressures.

As Paul pictures his readers, we recognize ourselves in his mirror. Here are Christian individuals troubled by the memory of a moral lapse. Here are Christians whose integrity has lost them a friend or a job. Here are Christian parents whose children are disappointing them. Here are Christians facing serious problems of health or physical limitation. Here are Christians made to feel like outsiders at home or at work because of their faith. Here are Christians burdened by the death of someone they feel should have lived or by the continued life of a senile relative or suffering child who they feel should have died. Here are Christians who feel God cannot care for them or their life would be less rough.

It is precisely people like this—people, in other words, like us—whom Paul is challenging. "What shall we say to these things? Don't just yield to the feelings of self-pity. Think—think—*think!*"

Journal: *Journal some of your own thoughtful responses to the hardships above.*

Wednesday

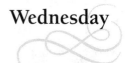

If God . . .

If God is for us, who can be against us?

ROMANS 8:31

$\mathcal{W}$ho is God? Paul speaks of the God of the Bible and of the gospel, the Lord Jehovah, "the compassionate and gracious God, slow to anger, abounding in love and faithfulness" (Exodus 34:6), the God whom "the only begotten Son, which is in the bosom of the Father, . . . hath declared" (John 1:18 KJV). This is the God who has spoken to announce his sovereignty: "I am God, and there is no other; I am God; and there is none like me. I make known the end from the beginning, from ancient times, what is still to come. I say: My purpose will stand, and I will do all that I please" (Isaiah 46:9-10). This is the God who showed his sovereignty by bringing Abraham out of Ur, Israel out of captivity in Egypt and later in Babylon, and Jesus out of the grave. This is the God who shows the same sovereignty still every time he raises a sinner to spiritual life out of spiritual death. This is the God who calls, justifies, and glorifies those whom from eternity he "predestined to be conformed to the likeness of his Son" (Romans 8:29).

Reflect: *Begin to memorize Romans 8:31-39. You will use it in the next several days.*

Thursday

God Is for Us

If God is for us, who can be against us?

ROMANS 8:31

*I*f God is "for us," what does that mean? The words "for us" declare God's covenant commitment. The promise to be "your God" which is, so to speak, the slogan of God's covenant with humans in all its forms (from Genesis 17:7 to Revelation 21:3) is a comprehensive promise that, when unpacked, proves to contain within itself all the "exceeding great and precious promises" (2 Peter 1:4 KJV) in which God has pledged himself to meet our needs.

This covenant relationship is the basis of all biblical religion. When worshipers say *"my* God" and God says *"my* people," covenant language is being talked. And the words "God is for us" are also covenant language. What is being proclaimed here is God's undertaking to uphold and protect us when people and circumstances are threatening, to provide for us as long as our earthly pilgrimage lasts, and to lead us finally into the full enjoyment of himself, however many obstacles may seem at present to stand in the way of our getting there.

The simple statement "God is for us" is in truth one of the richest and weightiest utterances that the Bible contains.

Journal: *Journal some of the significance of "God is for us" as you have experienced it—or hope to comprehend it.*

Friday   *Identity*

*When I am afraid, I will trust in you. In God,
whose word I praise, in God I trust; I will not
be afraid. What can mortal man do to me?*

PSALM 56:3-4

$\mathcal{P}$salm 56 helps answer the question who are the "us" whom
God is "for" of Romans 8:31. The psalmist displays three qualities that together mark out the true believer. First, he *praises,*
and what he praises is God's "word" (Psalm 56:4, 10). That is, he
attends to God's revelation and venerates God in it and according
to it, rather than indulging his own unchecked theological
fancies. Second, he *prays,* and the desire that prompts his prayer
is for communion with God as life's goal and end—"that I may
walk before God" (verse 13). Third, he *pays*—pays his vows, that
is, of faithfulness and thanksgiving (verse 12).

The praising, praying, thankful, faithful person has on him
the marks of being a child of God.

Reflect: *How can your identity as among the "us" that God is
"for" help you cope with some of your current fears?*

Saturday/Sunday

Them?

> *Be strong and courageous. Do not be*
> *afraid or discouraged. . . . With us is the L<small>ORD</small>*
> *our God to help us and to fight our battles.*

2 C<small>HRONICLES</small> 32:7-8

*H*aving asked the question "If God is for us, who can be against us?" in Romans 8:31, Paul says in effect, "Think! God is for you. Now reckon up who is against you and ask yourself how the two sides compare. Are you afraid of 'them'?"

Augustus Toplady voices the realization to which Paul's question seeks to lead us:

> A sovereign protector I have,
> Unseen, yet for ever at hand;
> Unchangeably faithful to save,
> Almighty to rule and command.
> He smiles, and may comfort abound;
> His grace as the dew shall descend,
> And walls of salvation surround
> The soul He delights to defend.

"Grasp this," says Paul; "Hold on to it. Let this certainty make its impact on you in relation to what you are up against at this very moment. You will find in thus knowing God as your sovereign protector, irrevocably committed to you in the covenant of grace, both freedom from fear and new strength for the fight."

Reflect: *Meditate on the words of 2 Chronicles 32. Bring to God the fears that passage suggests to you.*

Monday *God's Good Gifts*

> *He who did not spare his own Son,*
> *but gave him up for us all—how*
> *will he not also, along with him,*
> *graciously give us all things?*

ROMANS 8:32

*T*he thought expressed by Paul's second question of Romans 8 is that no good thing will finally be withheld from us.

Note what Paul implies about the costliness of our redemption. "He . . . did not spare his own Son." In saving us, God went to the limit. We cannot know what Calvary cost the Father any more than we can know what Jesus felt as he tasted the penalty due to our sins.

If the measure of love is what it gives, then there never was such love as God showed to sinners at Calvary, nor will any subsequent love gift to us cost God so much. So if God has already commended his love toward us in that while we were yet sinners Christ died for us (Romans 5:8), it is believable that he will go on to give us "all things" besides (8:32).

Most Christians know the fearful feeling that God may not have anything more for them beyond what they have already received. A thoughtful look at Calvary should banish this mood.

Pray: *Thank God for his gifts, past, present, and future, and the gift of Jesus Christ most of all.*

Tuesday

Christ Is for Us

He who did not spare his own Son,
but gave him up for us all . . .

ROMANS 8:32

*N*ote what Paul implies about the effectiveness of our redemption. "God," he says, "gave him up *for us all,*" and this fact is itself the guarantee that "all things" will be given us. The New Testament view is that the death of Christ has actually saved "us all"—all, that is to say, whom God foreknew and has called and justified and will in due course glorify.

Psychologically, faith is our own act, but the theological truth about it is that it is God's work in us. Our faith, our new relationship with God as believers, and all the divine gifts that are enjoyed within this relationship were all alike secured for us by Jesus' death on the cross. It ensured and guaranteed first the calling (the bringing to faith, through the gospel in the mind and the Holy Spirit in the heart), then the justification, and finally the glorification of all for whom, specifically and personally, Christ died. The saving purpose of God, from eternal election to final glory, is one.

Journal: *Reflect on the last sentence above and write a response.*

Wednesday

All Things

*How shall he not with him also
freely give us all things?*

ROMANS 8:32 KJV

*N*ote what Paul implies about the consequences of our redemption. God, he says, will with Christ give us "all things." What does that cover? Call, justification, and glorification (which in verse 30 includes everything from the new birth to the resurrection of the body). Paul's assurance that with Christ God will give us "all things" proclaims the adequacy of God as our sovereign benefactor, whose way with his servants leaves no ground for any sense or fear of real personal impoverishment at any stage.

This phrase has to do with knowing and enjoying God and not with anything else. The meaning of "he will give us all things" can be put thus: one day we shall see that nothing—literally nothing—that could have increased our eternal happiness has been denied us and that nothing—literally nothing—that could have reduced that happiness has been left with us. What higher assurance do we want than that?

Reflect: *Reread the statement beginning "One day we shall see that . . ." As you consider your current joys and pains, what might this statement mean for you?*

Thursday   *One God*

> *I am the LORD your God, who brought*
> *you out of Egypt, out of the land of slavery.*
> *You shall have no other gods before me.*

EXODUS 20:2-3

The Christian, like Israel at Sinai, faces the exclusive claim of the first commandment. God told Israel to serve him exclusively because he was worthy of their entire and exclusive trust. They were to bow to his absolute authority over them on the basis of confidence in his complete adequacy for them.

Now, if you are a Christian, you know what kind of life Christ calls you, as his disciple, to live. His own example and teaching in the Gospels make it abundantly clear. You are called to go through this world as a pilgrim, a mere temporary resident, traveling light. You are to be willing, as Christ directs, to give up material wealth and the security it provides and live in a way that involves you in poverty and loss of possessions. Having your treasure in heaven, you are not to budget for treasure on earth, nor for a high standard of living—you may well be required to forgo both. You are called to follow Christ, carrying your cross.

Journal: *What do you find challenging about the standard above? What do you find freeing about it?*

Friday

Needs

> *My God will meet all your needs according to his glorious riches in Christ Jesus.*

PHILIPPIANS 4:19

*W*e are unlike the Christians of New Testament times. The thought of "safety first" was not a drag on their enterprise as it is on ours. By being exuberant, unconventional, and uninhibited in living by the gospel, they turned their world upside down. You could not accuse us twenty-first-century Christians of doing anything like that.

Why are we so different? Whence comes the nervous, dithery, take-no-risks mood that mars so much of our discipleship? Why are we not free enough from fear and anxiety to allow ourselves to go full stretch in following Christ? Now let us call a spade a spade. The name of the game we are playing is *unbelief,* and Paul's "he will give us all things" (Romans 8:32) stands as an everlasting rebuke to us.

Paul is telling us that there is no ultimate loss or irreparable impoverishment to be feared. If God denies us something, it is only in order to make room for one or another of the things he has in mind. Are we, perhaps, still assuming that a person's life consists (partly, at any rate) in the things he possesses?

Journal: *Write your response to the final sentence above.*

Saturday/Sunday   *Risky Faith*

> *No good thing does the LORD withhold*
> *from those who walk uprightly.*

> **PSALM 84:11 RSV**

*W*hen it comes to cheerful self-abandonment in Christ's service, we dither. Why? Out of unbelief, pure and simple. Do we fear that God lacks strength or wisdom for fulfilling his declared purpose? Or do we fear that he is infirm of purpose and that, as good folks with good intentions sometimes let down their friends, so our God may fail to carry out his good intentions toward us? Or do we doubt his consistency, suspecting that he has "emerged" or "developed" or "died" in the interim between Bible times and our own?

Have you been holding back from a risky, costly course to which you know in your heart God has called you? Hold back no longer. Your God is faithful to you, and he is adequate for you. You will never need more than he can supply, and what he supplies, both materially and spiritually, will always be enough for the present. "No good thing does the LORD withhold from those who walk uprightly."

Pray: *Use the questions raised above for self-examination and prayer.*

Monday

Condemnation

Who will bring any charge against those whom God has chosen?

ROMANS 8:33

*T*here are two sorts of sick consciences, those that are not aware enough of sin and those that are not aware enough of pardon, and it is to the second sort that Paul is ministering now. He knows how easily the conscience of a Christian under pressure can grow morbid, particularly when that Christian's nose is rubbed, as Romans 7:24-25 would rub it, in the reality of continued sin and failure. Paul speaks directly to the fear (to which no Christian is a total stranger) that present justification may be no more than provisional—that it may one day be lost by reason of the imperfections of one's Christian life. But Paul denies emphatically that any lapses now can endanger our justified status. The reason, he says in effect, is simple: nobody is in a position to get God's verdict reviewed!

Reflect: *Who is most likely to condemn you—family, church, yourself? What do you find in Romans 8 to help you deal with that sense of condemnation?*

Tuesday

Love's Embrace

*Who shall separate us
from the love of Christ?*

ROMANS 8:35

*H*uman love, for all its power in other ways, cannot ensure that what is desired for the beloved will actually happen, as multitudes of star-crossed lovers and heartbroken parents know. But the love Paul speaks of is love that saves, and the New Testament will not allow anyone to suppose that this divine love embraces him unless he has come as a sinner to Jesus and has learned to say to Jesus with Thomas, "My Lord and my God!" (John 20:28). But once a person has truly given himself up to the Lord Jesus, he never need feel the uncertainty of the cartoonist's lady who murmurs as she puffs at the thistledown, "He loves me—he loves me not—."

It is the privilege of all Christians to know for certain that God loves us immutably and that nothing can at any time part us from that love or come between us and the final enjoyment of its fruits.

Journal: *What are some of the forces that threaten your relationship with God? Acknowledge these threats in writing and then respond from your protected place within the strength of God's love.*

Wednesday

God's Generosity

The LORD, The LORD God, merciful and gracious, longsuffering, and abundant in goodness and truth . . .

EXODUS 34:6 KJV

*W*ithin the cluster of God's moral perfections there is one in particular to which the term "goodness" points. This is the quality of generosity. *Generosity* means a disposition to give to others in a way that has no mercenary motive and is not limited by what the recipients deserve but consistently goes beyond it. God is "abundant in goodness"—*ultro bonus,* as Latin-speaking theologians used to put it.

Theologians of the Reformed school use the New Testament word "grace" (free favor) to cover every act of divine generosity, of whatever kind. Hence they distinguish between, on the one hand, the *common grace* of creation, preservation, and all the blessings of this life and, on the other hand, the *special grace* manifested in the economy of salvation. The point of the contrast between *common* and *special* being that all benefit from the former, but not all are touched by the latter. The biblical way of putting this distinction would be to say that God is good to all in some ways and to some in all ways.

Journal: *Spend about ten minutes listing as many of God's kindnesses in your life as come to mind. Then note beside each whether it represents his common grace or his special grace. Thank him for both.*

Thursday

Glad Heart

I keep the LORD always before me; . . . I shall not be moved. Therefore my heart is glad, and my soul rejoices.

PSALM 16:8-9 RSV

*K*nowing God means becoming a disciple of Jesus, the living Savior who is "there" today, calling the needy to himself as he did in Galilee in the days of his flesh. Knowing God, in other words, involves *faith*—assent, consent, commitment—and faith expresses itself in prayer and obedience. "The best measure of a spiritual life," said Oswald Chambers, "is not its ecstasies, but its obedience." Now finally we learn that a person who knows God will live in Romans 8, exulting with Paul in the adequacy of God. And here we have to stop, for this is as high in the knowledge of God as we can go this side of glory.

Where has all this led us? To the very heart of biblical religion. We have been brought to the point where David's prayer and profession in Psalm 16 may become our own: "Thou art my Lord; I have no good apart from thee" (verses 1-2 RSV).

Pray: *Read all of Psalm 16, pausing now and then to add your own prayer of worship.*

Friday   *Finale*

> *I am convinced that neither death nor life,*
> *neither angels nor demons, neither the present*
> *nor the future, nor any powers, neither height*
> *nor depth, nor anything else in all creation,*
> *will be able to separate us from the love of*
> *God that is in Christ Jesus our Lord.*

ROMANS 8:38-39

*P*aul proclaims a triumphant declaration in Romans 8:38-39, in which the heartbeat of Christian assurance is heard. As J. B. Phillips's translation puts it, "I am absolutely convinced that there is nothing in death or life, in the realm of spirits or superhuman powers, in the world as it is or the world as it shall be, in the forces of the universe, in heights or depths—nothing in all creation that can separate us from the love of God in Christ Jesus our Lord." God is adequate as our keeper. The love of God holds us fast. The power of God keeps us believing as well as keeps us safe through believing.

Your faith will not fail while God sustains it. You are not strong enough to fall away while God is resolved to hold you.

Journal: *Meditate on each phrase of Romans 8:38-39 and write a prayer of response.*

Saturday/Sunday   *Path and Prize*

*I consider everything a loss
compared to the surpassing greatness
of knowing Christ Jesus my Lord.*

PHILIPPIANS 3:8

*H*uman love relationships—between child and parent, wife and husband, or friend and friend—are ends in themselves, having their value and joy in themselves. The same is true of our knowledge of the God who loves us, the God whose love is seen in Jesus. Paul wrote in effect, "I count everything sheer loss, because all is far outweighed by the gain of knowing Christ Jesus my Lord, for whose sake I did in fact lose everything." As the old hymn puts it, "Christ is the path, and Christ the prize."

The purpose of our relationship with God in Christ is the perfecting of the relationship itself. How could it be otherwise, when it is a love relationship? So God is adequate in this sense, that in knowing him fully we shall find ourselves fully satisfied, needing and desiring nothing more.

Reflect: *Knowing Christ is both the path and the prize of the Christian life. Reflect on what this means for your present and your future.*

Monday 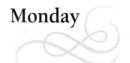 *Fighting Fear*

> *In all these things we are more than
> conquerors through him who loved us.*

ROMANS 8:37

*I*n Romans 8 Paul is countering fear—fear, this time, of the unknown, whether in terms of unprecedented suffering (Romans 8:35-36) or of a horrific future ("the world as it shall be") or of cosmic forces that one cannot measure or master ("height" and "depth" in verse 39 are technical astrological terms for mysterious cosmic powers). The focus of fear is the effect these things might have on one's fellowship with God, by overwhelming both reason and faith and so destroying sanity and salvation together.

In an age like ours (not so different in this respect from Paul's!), all Christians, especially the more imaginative, know something of this fear. It is the Christian version of the existential angst at the prospect of personal destruction. But, says Paul, we must fight this fear, for the bogey is unreal. Nothing, literally nothing, can separate us from the love of God. "In all these things we are more than conquerors through him who loved us."

Journal: *What are some of your current fears? Recite aloud Romans 8:35-39 as God's challenge to those fears. Write your reflections on this subject.*

Tuesday

Faith Song

> *Since we have a great high priest who has gone through the heavens, Jesus the Son of God, let us hold firmly to the faith we profess.*

HEBREWS 4:14

*W*hen Paul and Silas sat in the stocks in the Philippian jail, they found themselves so exultant that at midnight they began to sing. This is how those who know God's sovereign love will always find themselves when the harrowing things are actually upon them.

Once again Augustus Toplady leads us in a hymn:

From whence this fear and unbelief? Hath not the Father
    put to grief
His spotless Son for me?

And will the righteous Judge of men condemn me for that
    debt of sin
Which, Lord, was charged on Thee?

Complete atonement Thou has made, and to the utmost
    farthing paid
Whate'er Thy people owed;

Nor can His wrath on me take place, if sheltered in
    Thy righteousness
And sprinkled with Thy blood.

Pray: *Using the hymn and Scripture above, bring to God any nagging fears and unbelief you may have. Pray also your faith and your thanksgiving.*

Wednesday   *Knowing God*

I know whom I have believed, and am
convinced that he is able to guard what
I have entrusted to him for that day.

2 TIMOTHY 1:12

The climax of our book has now been reached. We set out to see
what it means to know God. We found that the God who is
"there" for us to know is the God of the Bible, the God of Romans,
the God revealed in Jesus, the Three-in-One of historic Christian
teaching. We realized that knowing him starts with knowing
about him, so we studied his revealed character and ways and
came to know something of his goodness and severity, his wrath
and his grace. As we did so, we learned to reevaluate ourselves
as fallen creatures, not strong and self-sufficient as we once sup-
posed but weak, foolish, and indeed bad, heading not for Utopia
but for hell unless grace intervenes. Also, we saw that knowing
God involves a personal relationship whereby you give yourself
to God on the basis of his promise to give himself to you.
Knowing God means asking his mercy and resting on his undertaking to forgive sinners for Jesus' sake.

Reflect: *How has "knowing God" through this book shaped your*
thinking, your worship, your living out of your faith? What ques-
tions would you like to explore further?

Thursday

Giving Thanks

Give thanks to the Lord, for he is good.

Psalm 107:1

*T*he classical exposition of God's goodness is Psalm 107. Here, to enforce his summons to "give thanks to the Lord, for he is good" (Psalm 107:1), the psalmist gives four examples of how people "cried out" (verses 6, 13, 19, 28). The first example is of God redeeming the helpless from their enemies and leading them to find a home. The second is of God delivering from "darkness and the shadow of death" (verse 14 KJV) those whom he had himself brought into this condition because of their rebellion. The third is of God healing the diseases with which he had chastened "fools" who disregarded him. The fourth is of God protecting voyagers by stilling the storm. Each episode ends with the refrain "Let them give thanks to the Lord for his unfailing love and his wonderful deeds for men" (verses 8, 15, 21, 31). The whole psalm is a majestic panorama of the operations of divine goodness transforming human lives.

Reflect: *Review the many examples of God's goodness in Psalm 107. What similar events in your own life lead you to give thanks?*

Friday

Joyful Still

Though the fig tree does not bud
and there are no grapes on the vines,
though the olive crop fails
and the fields produce no food,
though there are no sheep in the pen
and no cattle in the stalls,
yet I will rejoice in the LORD,
I will be joyful in God my Savior.

HABAKKUK 3:17-18

By knowing God, we may say with Habakkuk in the face of economic ruin or any other deprivation: "Though the fig tree does not bud, . . . yet I will rejoice in the LORD." Happy the person who can say these things and mean them!

We have been brought to the point where we can grasp the truth in descriptions of the Christian's life in terms of "victory" and "Jesus satisfies." Used naively, this language could mislead, for the "victory" is not yet the end of the war. Nonetheless these phrases point to the link between knowledge of God on the one hand and human fulfillment on the other. When we speak of the adequacy of God, it is this link that we highlight, and this link is of the essence of Christianity. Those who know God in Christ have found the secret of true freedom and true humanity.

Journal: *Write your own paraphrase of Habakkuk 3:17-19, working in as illustrations things that threaten your own sense of security.*

Saturday/Sunday

Secure

Thou hast said, "Seek ye my face."
My heart says to thee, "Thy face, LORD,
do I seek." Hide not thy face from me.

PSALM 27:8-9 RSV

*W*e have been brought to the point where we both can and must get our life priorities straight. So many in our day seem to have been distracted from what was, is, and always will be the true priority for every human being—learning to know God in Christ. Perhaps they need as a motive the joy that springs from knowing what Augustus Toplady clearly knew:

> My name from the palms of His hands eternity will not erase;
> Impressed on His heart it remains in marks of indelible grace;
> Yes, I to the end shall endure, as sure as the earnest is given;
> More happy, but not more secure, the glorified spirits in
> heaven!

Pray: *Pray your response to God for what you have gained and what you have yet to gain through your experience of this book.*

Index of Hymns